On Bonfires,
Butlins and
Being Welsh

On Bonfires, Butlins and Being Welsh

GROWING UP IN PWLLHELI
IN THE '50s AND '60s

JOS SIMON

First impression: 2022

© Copyright Jos Simon and Y Lolfa Cyf., 2022

The contents of this book are subject to copyright, and may
not be reproduced by any means, mechanical or electronic,
without the prior, written consent of the publishers.

Cover design: Y Lolfa
Cover image: Simon van de Put

ISBN: 978 1 80099 187 3

Published and printed in Wales
on paper from well-maintained forests by
Y Lolfa Cyf., Talybont, Ceredigion SY24 5HE
website www.ylolfa.com
e-mail ylolfa@ylolfa.com
tel 01970 832 304
fax 832 782

Contents

Map of the Llŷn Peninsula

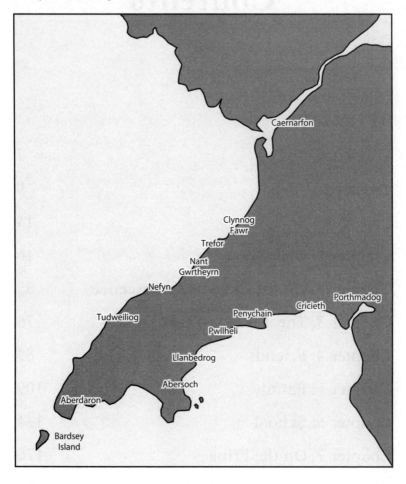

Foreword

I WAS TYING myself into hopeless knots compiling a collection of school day memories shared by members of 'my' Facebook group, when Jos sent me a copy of his typescript, *On Bonfires, Butlins and Being Welsh*, and invited me to write a Foreword to his upcoming book. Hence I read *On Bonfires, Butlins and Being Welsh* with relief mixed with admiration. Social media may be an ideal medium for sharing tales, fact-checking and swapping photographs with others, but it is less than ideal for creating a work of reference and does little to satisfy the social historian, librarian or even the gossip among us.

Jos and I sat at desks in the same grammar school classrooms, were taught by the same teachers and joined the great Welsh diaspora, albeit a decade apart. Unlike Jos, I returned to live locally, attended sporadic school reunions and even published a website for our year. But as our fortieth anniversary approached, I decided we needed to cast our net a little wider, so I founded the *Ysgolion Pwllheli & District Schools* (YPDS) Facebook group in 2013.

Jos stumbled across YPDS early, but did not stand out from the crowd until November 2019, when his post recalling the plotting and scheming surrounding bonfire nights in the 1960s went off with a bang. This and subsequent posts about growing up in Pwllheli were all lapped up, and ensuing feedback spurred him to dig deeper into the recesses of his carpet-bag memory. YPDS was a sounding-board and resource in equal measure, with responses adding much meat or gentle correction to tales.

My congenital bossiness with a librarian-cum-historian's desire for orderliness provided the bare bones for Jos to build upon, with group members proving themselves as willing collaborators.

It was brilliant timing when Jos Simon burst onto the scene, with his vivid schoolboy memories, just as we all slid into morose contemplation of our own mortality through the first plague year. *On Bonfires, Butlins and Being Welsh* is a universal tale of a small-town boy in and of his times, coloured by the kaleidoscope of hindsight.

Diolch – thank you, Jos, and the many others who have made this a rollicking good read. You have done Pwllheli and its many characters proud. However it is worth noting that Pwllheli also did you proud, Jos. To paraphrase: you can take the boy out of Wales, but you can't take Wales out of the boy.

Janet Kaiser
Criccieth
December 2021

Preface

I WAS ONE of a group of kids born and raised just after the Second World War in the small seaside town of Pwllheli, which sits on the pretty south coast of the Llŷn Peninsula in north-west Wales. If you think of the outline of Wales as a pig wearing a flat cap heading a ball – not the most flattering of images, I'll grant you – Llŷn is the peak of the cap.

We were feral baby-boomers who ran wild around the town and the countryside in the 1950s. We benefited from a freedom to roam typical of the time, yet unthinkable today. Although rules inside our homes were often draconian, in the wider community we could do what we liked – out of sight was out of mind. Adults, when they noticed us at all, were indulgent, as long as we kept our heads down and stayed out of their way.

As we grew up we morphed into a group of adolescents whose struggle with rampant hormones, emotional trial-and-error relationships, the search for ourselves, and the butting of heads with significant adults was typical, I'm sure, of any teenagers in any society at any time in history. That this was the 1960s, one of the most studied and talked-about decades of modern times, has perhaps made us more prone than usual to nostalgia, and to that cocky assumption, which later generations find insufferable, that our growing up was uniquely blessed.

Then, as adolescence shaded into maturity, some of us stayed in Pwllheli and got jobs; others moved away, in my case to England and university.

Like many who left Pwllheli, I returned often, on my own

as a student, with my girlfriend then wife and, in due course, children and grandchildren. Finally, as my parents, my aunts and uncles, and some of my friends died, as surviving friends dispersed, the visits became sporadic, and I lost touch. The whole bubble of my childhood and adolescence floated off into the past. I lived in various parts of England during thirty years of teaching, and after retirement ranged widely across the UK and Europe following a late-blooming travel-writing career.

With age came time to think. The responsibilities of parenthood slowly dissipated as the kids grew up, whilst others towards ageing parents were sadly short-lived. I got older, with less to look forward to, more to look back on. In the words of the song:

'Now that I'm old and I'm ready to go,

I got to thinking what happened a long time ago.'

Though I'm really not. Ready to go, that is.

From Frankie Vaughan to Socrates. The Greek philosopher said that 'The unexamined life is not worth living.' And that's what you do when you get to where we boomers are today – feeling increasingly irrelevant, facing extinction. You examine your life.

Before continuing, it would seem sensible, for the benefit of those who don't know our corner of north-west Wales, to sketch in the background of Pwllheli and its hinterland, to set the scene. I'll use the past tense. This is what it was like as I remember it, not necessarily what it's like today.

Pwllheli and the Llŷn Peninsula

Pwllheli was the principal market town of the Llŷn Peninsula. Thanks to the Gulf Stream on one side and the mountains of Snowdonia on the other, it had a mild climate with, to the bitter regret of us kids, little snow. The people of the town traditionally worked in seafaring, ship building, farming and tourism, together with the professions and businesses that served them.

Pwllheli shouldn't be thought of, though, as sufficient unto itself. It was part of what was in effect a single community – that of the Llŷn Peninsula. It was the transport hub and main focus for retail, entertainment, education and local government. It was not, however, the only centre of population – the smaller towns of Cricieth, Llanbedrog, Abersoch, Aberdaron, Nefyn, Morfa Nefyn and Trefor, together with a host of smaller villages and hamlets, made up a coherent community with a common accent, culture and history.

Since the end of the Second World War, Pwllheli has changed very little. As recently as the most recent census, eighty per cent of its inhabitants spoke Welsh. Its population, steady at four thousand or so, was largely made up of families who'd been there for generations, with little dilution by incomers from the rest of the UK or abroad. It therefore provided us Pwllheli kids, and those of the surrounding towns, villages and farms, with a secure and stable environment in which to grow up.

Geography is history

In the past, community depended on proximity. To take part in the life of a town like Pwllheli, or an area like Llŷn, you pretty much had to live there. This was fine for the twenty thousand or so residents of Pwllheli and the Llŷn Peninsula, but the rest of us – exiles, dotted around the UK, Europe and the world – were condemned to a lifetime of 'hiraeth' (longing).

Then came the internet, and more specifically, social media.

Facebook provided the means whereby, using modern technology, our close-knit small town and village communities – their pubs, local schools, churches and chapels, the shops and all the rest – could be recreated with no face-to-face contact whatsoever. All it needed was for community-minded folk with a bit of tech-savvy and a willingness to give up some of their time to set up Facebook groups like *Ysgolion Pwllheli & District*

11

Schools, *Old Pictures of Pwllheli*, and *Hiraeth Gogledd Cymru*. God bless them all.

So today it really is true that 'geography is history'.

The book

Some time ago my son posted on Facebook photos I'd taken in Pwllheli in the mid-1970s. We couldn't believe the outpouring of stories and reminiscences that the pictures triggered. It set me thinking about growing up in that part of north Wales in the 1950s and '60s, and how there was so much worth remembering and recording. So I started posting my own memories from those times in a Facebook group dedicated to those of us who were brought up in the area. The group was, and is, called *Ysgolion Pwllheli & District Schools*.

As the memories built up, a number of group members suggested that it might be worthwhile collecting these essentially ephemeral Facebook posts into a book, to preserve them more permanently. Initially my response was that it was all just a bit of fun, of no interest to anybody but alas diminishing number of us who lived in that place, at that time. Old fogeys reminiscing about the distant past. Maudlin nostalgia. Who'd want to read about that, I thought.

But as I read back over the posts and the outpouring of anecdotes and opinions, the banter and jokes, the reconnection of people who had lost touch perhaps half a century ago, I started to think that yes, indeed, here was something of value. Here was a chance to record memories of our friends, our families, our teachers, our town, our peninsula, our culture. Surely it was worth the time and effort needed to preserve it?

The posts were, after all, already written. It only needed the addition of a summary of the comments and the book would write itself! What could be easier?

I set to. I printed off the original posts and added, where relevant, postscripts to include some of the comments. I needed to shuffle them into some sort of coherent order. This proved harder than it sounds. I tried doing it by theme, but it looked to be much like life itself – just one damned thing after another. A chronological approach perhaps? Again, no dice – organising memories turned out to be like herding cats.

I finally settled on a mishmash of rough chronology and broad themes:

- Childhood
- On the cusp of adolescence
- The teenage years
- Friends
- Family
- School
- On the fringes
- Leaving Pwllheli
- Wales and the Welsh
- Then and now

So that's how this book was born.

Prologue

WITH THE DEATH of my mother in 2008 my last family tie with Pwllheli was broken. Despite a flurry of visits after her death, to do with her will and getting her house ready to be put on the market, it seemed likely that from then on I wouldn't be seeing much of my home town.

On one of these last visits I climbed to the top of the Garn, the hill overlooking Pwllheli, taking the route up Salem Terrace and past what used to be the grammar school's hockey field. Standing on the summit next to the trig point, I looked outwards across the town and the harbour to Gimblet Rock and the sea, westwards to the headlands of Carreg-y-Defaid and Llanbedrog, and the two St Tudwal's Islands, and eastwards along the sweep of the bay towards Penychain and Cricieth. I could see the whole of my childhood and adolescence laid out below me, like a map. There was the house in Llŷn Street where I was born and raised, my primary (Penlleiniau) and secondary (Ysgol Ramadeg Pwllheli) schools, the railway station from which I left for university, the church where I and both my children were christened, and where I attended my brother's wedding and the funerals of both my parents.

As I descended from the Garn, taking the alternative route via the top of Llŷn Street, I felt a fleeting sadness, but then thought no more about it. My childhood and youth were fading into the past where, surely, they belonged.

Ten years later, I'm not sure why, my memories decided

that they were not going to 'go gentle into that good night', and exploded into my consciousness in full and vivid colour. I started to write them down, and to post them on Facebook.

CHAPTER 1

Childhood

GROWING UP IN a town like Pwllheli in the 1950s and '60s, there wasn't much to do and an awful lot of time to do it in. So, when you were too young to hang out in coffee bars, and much too young for pubs (unless you were outside with a bottle of pop and a packet of crisps), you were forced to spend a lot of evenings and weekends and school holidays just roaming around the town and the surrounding area. Think *Last of the Summer Wine* but with kids instead of pensioners. Such was the dearth of facilities that we had to visit the rubbish tip, tour the shops or the coin-in-the-slot machines, watch people work, massacre blameless animals, or risk our lives, just for something to do. Also, in fairness, rove beautiful countryside, play in streams and woodland, climb rocks and trees, make dens in great swathes of bracken, and enjoy some of the best beaches in the UK. This, then, was the background to our childhood.

Bonfire night

During the weeks leading up to Guy Fawkes night, bonfires would grow in different parts of Pwllheli. Ours was on the Garn. Built largely of branches, bracken and gorse, it burned brightly, even ferociously, but all too quickly.

As it died down, the older boys developed a way of occupying themselves for the rest of the evening. They nailed tin cans to the end of stout sticks, filled the cans with bits of cloth soaked in meths, and lit them. Then, holding these improvised torches aloft, they would descend on the town, followed by hordes of little kids like me, visiting each rival bonfire in turn, swearing, throwing bangers and being generally obnoxious.

At the time I thought this very exciting. Now a grandfather in my seventies, I'm mortified – what a bunch of yahoos we all were!

Postscript

When I wrote this post, I could, of course, reflect only on my own experience as a small boy who was part of the 'Garn' bonfire gang. My assumption was that we were wreaking havoc on the peaceful, law-abiding bonfires of the town at Wembley, Gadlys, Penmount, Morfa'r Garreg and South Beach.

The comments added to my post showed me how wrong I was.

Pwllheli, in the weeks leading up to 5 November, was a war zone, a seething cauldron of guerrilla action as rival bonfire-gangs scoured the town and its hinterland, competing for old furniture, mattresses, crates, discarded tyres, cardboard boxes, anything combustible.

As the bonfires grew, so did the rivalry. Each gang would try to set fire to the half-built bonfires of their enemies, whilst putting in place measures to combat their rivals' attempts to set fire to their own.

Defensive moves included, apparently, all-night sentry duty at bedroom windows overlooking the bonfire site, keeping materials safely locked in grandparents' garages until the last minute, even throwing up defensive earthworks and digging trenches.

Attacks involved secretly infiltrating enemy territory (wearing camo? with burnt-cork-blackened faces?) to destroy rival bonfires. Picture it – little guerrillas crawling commando-style (from under a coal lorry, in one instance) towards the enemy site, hearts set on sabotage, only to be thwarted by tumbling into the defensive ditch put there to pre-empt such attacks.

Despite all precautions, sometimes the attackers got through and the balloon, or in this case the bonfire, went up. Then Plan B sprang into action. Gangs of kids scoured neighbourhoods for replacement materials, or sallied onto Allt Bartu or The Jungle in Talcymerau with axes and ropes to gather branches and saplings and gorse. Everybody, adults and children, pulled together in a spirit of common endeavour, and invariably a new bonfire and Guy would be ready for sacrifice by 5 November.

Even then it wasn't all plain sailing. On the night, adults had to deal with Catherine wheels that failed to spin but hung, spitting forlornly, on their nails, Roman candles that fizzled out, rockets that refused to leave their milk bottles. In between, they had to chase little boys who'd been throwing bangers and jumping-jacks up little girls' skirts, and extinguish small fires lit by the sparks pouring out of the heart of the bonfire.

Looking at this, then, from the perspective of a member of the Garn bonfire gang, I needn't have worried that our puny raids might have spoilt things for bonfires in other parts of the town. All hell was already breaking loose. Far from ruining things for the peaceful family gatherings of my imagination, I think we were lucky to get away with our lives!

A football match

I recently came across a diary I started when I was eight years old. Its only entry offered a vivid glance into what it was like to be a kid in Pwllheli in the 1950s.

Some of us at Penlleiniau had gotten together with our contemporaries at Troed-yr-Allt – the only other primary school in town – to arrange a football match. This was early in January. The venue was to be the field between South Beach and West End – the building of Ffordd-y-Mela, joining the two beach communities, still lay in the future.

The memories sparked by the diary are patch
vague recollection of walking up Cardiff Road
towards the field of combat with my football boo
together, slung around my neck, my breath smoking in the
freezing air. I don't remember much about the match itself.
I have no idea who provided the ball. I assume the goalposts
were piles of coats. We certainly didn't have a referee.

However, I do remember the huge flat cow pats that dotted
the pitch – hard and gnarled like tree bark on the outside but,
when stepped on, green and slippery underneath. Sliding
tackles lubricated by foul-smelling cow dung, though effective,
I'd prefer to forget.

The short diary entry for me encapsulated the whole 1950s
ethos of kids cracking on to organise their own leisure, with
no input from, or supervision by, adults. The last line seemed
particularly poignant: 'We were a goal behind but scored twice
when the moon went behind the clouds.'

Shops

It's remarkable how much time, and how little money, we kids
spent in shops.

In pre-Internet days, each family had its own selection of
go-to retailers. The Simon family lived towards the bottom
of Llŷn Street, so ours tended to be in the centre of town.
Thinking about those childhood shops, it surprised me how
many memories they kicked loose.

In the High Street:

Woolworths: A two-minute walk from our house, and
useful for a wide range of household goods, sweets, toys,
records and magazines. Also, I'm ashamed to say, a target
for competitive small-boy shoplifting, usually, for some
reason, little friction-driven cars. Surely the statute of
limitations applies to pilfering? If not, I made this up.

Peacocks: A sort of poor man's Woolworths. Everything

was cheap, and the staff had obviously been trained to warn off urchins like us with a stern 'Don't touch!' This was so unvarying that we would deliberately provoke the warning by touching something, go into fits of giggles when the girl (and it was always a girl) duly obliged, then run off thunderously – the wooden floors in Peacocks were curiously hollow, and the shop was always almost empty.

Thorntons: We didn't have much use for Thorntons (fruit? veg? flowers? I don't think so). But one of our friends was the daughter of the owners, so we were sometimes invited to lounge about and take refreshments at the back of the shop. It was here, after youth club in the Church Hall, that our friend, ashen-faced, came in and told us that President Kennedy had been assassinated. Years later, Thorntons was a godsend when I'd forgotten my mother's birthday – a quick phone call, an Interflora delivery, and Bob's your uncle. Expensive, but worth every penny.

Williams 80: For general food supplies and groceries, most memorable for the way in which it would flood the High Street with glorious coffee smells when they were grinding the beans in their big enamel and chrome mill. It was to Williams 80 that I was sent on most of my errands by my mother. When I asked her why she was such a loyal customer, she simply said, 'They were good to us during the war.' Whether this was by extending credit, or related to under-the-counter off-ration shenanigans, I've no idea. Mum's loyalty didn't cut any ice when it came to Mr Williams's daughter, though. She was very pretty, and my brother wanted to ask her out, but any romance was nipped in the bud by her dad, who regarded Jeff as a Teddy Boy and a ne'er-do-well.

The Tower Hotel: Run by Tommy Jones, of Everton, Wales and now Pwllheli and District. The Tower didn't figure much in our thoughts until we were over eighteen, when we started to use the cocktail lounge on the first floor.

The only time I entered the main hotel was during my cousin Jill's wedding reception, when my father surprised me (you never expect your dad to be able to do stuff like that) by giving an excellent, and very funny, speech. He was standing in for father-of-the-bride Uncle Dick, who couldn't make it from south Wales.

Boots the Chemist: It stays mostly in my memory because a group of us helped ourselves to free samples of tablets in the shop. I don't know what they were for but, a few hours later, they turned our pee a deep dark blue. It eventually wore off but didn't half give us a fright. What were we thinking? Boots was also the source of sulphur, which we would buy and set alight (though why we did this escapes me), and Plaster of Paris, useful for taking impressions of birds' feet in the snow. On the very rare occasions, that is, when it did snow in Pwllheli.

W.H. Smiths: For books and comics, and also rubbers, rulers, pencils, pens – all the stuff that, for my grandchildren, turn a visit to Rymans into a treat. I'll talk later about the stockroom, down an alley next to the shop.

James the Barber: Favoured by old men (and my father). I went there until, at thirteen, I rebelled and went to John the Barber (see below). James wasn't a good advert for his services – he was bald. Unlike John, who had a fine head of black hair.

In Penlan Street:

John the Barber: Favoured by young men and likely lads. Just off Penlan Street, next to the entrance to the Liberal Club, John knew what 'DAs' and 'Italian crews' were. Unlike James, who gave you a short-back-and-sides whatever you asked for. As you were waiting your turn, men would tap on the small side-window, which John would open, say, 'Something for the weekend?', then palm out a small packet in exchange for money. I still have no idea what this was all about.

Halfway down (I don't remember the name. Now, I think, called Llŷn Angling): A shop whose main business was selling leather goods, but to us was where we bought fishing line (wound onto wooden frames), hooks and lead weights (for crab fishing in the harbour) and thick, square-section elastic (for making catapults). Two popular childhood pastimes, right there, more of which later.

In Gaol Street:

West End Stores: An old-fashioned ironmongers', an Aladdin's cave of pocket-knives and daggers, much too expensive for the likes of us. Used, though, for nails and screws and, in my case, our family's supply of paraffin.

Kampala: Run by a lovely woman with two sons – one a ranger in Snowdonia National Park, the other a joiner who worked next to and behind the shop. It was here, in the early 1950s, I used to take my ration coupons to buy my weekly allowance of two ounces of sweets.

In Station Square:

John Summers: For sports goods. A group of us bought a rugby ball on the never-never, pooling our pocket money. When it was my turn to keep it at home, I had to own up to my parents that we'd bought it on hire-purchase. They were not pleased. Mum: 'You should always live within your means. I've never bought anything that I couldn't pay cash for.' Me: 'What about the new washing machine?' Mum: 'That's different.'

In the Maes:

Bodawen Café: Mainly for ice cream. Somebody has mentioned that there was a juke box, but I don't recall one. I do remember Horlicks, whipped with a special branded machine and served in mugs with filled-in handles.

Ensors: Mr Ensor repaired shoes, and his shop flooded that part of the Maes with the lovely smell of leather.

The Market: Every Wednesday, stalls ousted parked cars.

For all sorts of goods, including jeans, coats, tools, and Welsh rock. It was sometimes a pleasure to just listen to the stallholders' patter and fight for the pencils they threw into the crowd.

In the future, it's hard to imagine on-line shopping generating similar memories.

Postscript

In the comments it was pointed out that my remembered shops were very small-boy orientated. I defended myself, reasonably I thought, by pointing out that I was indeed a small boy. So clothes shops, butchers, bakeries and the like feature little in my reminiscences. This led me to the further thought that a list of memorable shops compiled separately by boys and girls would reflect gender stereotyping in 1950s and '60s Pwllheli. I offer this, free of charge, as a possible area of study to any would-be PhD student.

Another response to the post listed by name over a hundred Pwllheli shops. Whilst not all had existed simultaneously, it was still an impressive total for so small a town. Just reading through the names provoked paroxysms of nostalgia.

Finally, two comments indicated the dark criminal underbelly of youth culture in the town:

- The pinching of an apple from the pavement display of the greengrocers in what used to be Pwllheli's gaol provoked only an indulgent smile from the shopkeeper when the conscience-stricken thief tearfully returned to confess.

- The surreptitious taking of five sweets in a four-for-a-penny display was compensated for when the (different) conscience-stricken delinquent took only three sweets on her next visit to the shop.

As I said in the original post, it's difficult to imagine Amazon provoking such an outpouring of memories.

Coin-in-the-slot machines

As backup for when the shops were shut – which they usually were outside strict opening hours – Pwllheli boasted a huge array of coin-in-the-slot machines:

- Cigarette machines. The one that stuck in my mind was outside Bodawen Café in the Maes, but I'm sure there were many others. They were essential for nicotine addicts caught out-of-hours without cigarettes.

- The milk and orange-juice machine outside John Summers in Station Square. Handy for drinkers after closing-time tortured by a post-session thirst, or for caffeine-heads who'd run out of milk for their coffee.

- In the railway station, a machine which dispensed platform tickets, and a huge red contraption which allowed you, for a penny, to emboss words on an aluminium strip. The former was essential if you wanted to see friends or relatives onto the train and the ticket office was closed. I'm not sure what the latter was for – perhaps making labels for luggage. We kids, if we had a spare penny, would use it to print rude words.

- Massive scales for weighing yourself in Woolworths, situated between the two doors into the shop. Most people, I presume, didn't have scales at home. Still, not sure what the purpose of the Woolworths scales was – you could hardly jump out of the bath and, swathed in a towel, sprint down to Woolworths to check how the diet was going.

- A stamp-book dispenser outside the Post Office. In those days stamps were only available in Post Offices – ordinary newsagents weren't allowed to sell them. So stamp machines were essential if the Post Office was closed and your letter was urgent.

- A Beech Nut chewing-gum vending machine halfway down Gaol Street. I can't imagine why anyone would be in urgent need of chewing gum. There was an arrow on the dispensing knob, and if it was pointing towards you, you got an extra free packet of gum. This was why you'd sometimes see a group of small boys lounging nonchalantly next to the machine, keeping a sharp eye on the knob.

- A word needs to be said here about phone boxes. Before the introduction of STD in the 1960s, making a call required you to feed money into the slot (four old pennies, I think). Then, if your call went through you pressed Button A to be connected, and if it didn't go through, you pressed Button B to get your money back. Many people forgot to press Button B. So we kids would do a tour of the town's phone boxes, pressing Button B in each one. Often this was a waste of time, but sometimes you hit the jackpot. The phone box outside the Town Hall was, for some reason, the one that paid out most frequently.

There were, then, lots of vending machines dotted around the town. So, if out-of-hours you urgently needed one of the necessities of life (fags, milk, stamps, chewing gum), wanted to see somebody off on a train, post an important letter or felt an irresistible urge to find out how much you weighed, you were still OK. Except, come to think of it, getting weighed – if Woolworths was shut, you were jiggered.

Postscript

Two memories here of malfunctioning coin-operated machines leading to considerable glee and profit. One, a petrol pump at Glandon Garage, which continued to deliver fuel long past the 50p's worth it was designed to allow. This must have been after 1971, when the currency was decimalised. People from miles around drove there as the news spread. Another was the cigarette machine outside Bodawen which continued to shell out free packets of fags after the initial coins had been fed into the slot.

An explanation was also offered, by the grandson of police Chief Inspector Shaw who would know about such things, for the fact that the Town Hall phone box was, as he called it, the 'jackpot king'. It was equidistant between two of the town's most popular pubs – The Tower and the Penlan Fawr. One only has to imagine maudlin young men after a few drinks phoning their sweethearts, or older drinkers calling their wives to make excuses, and in each case, when they failed to get through, in their distress forgetting to press button B.

Saturday matinée

Pwllheli's children's matinée took place every Saturday afternoon at the Palladium cinema. As I recall, the programme would include a cartoon (for example *Tom and Jerry*) or other short (say *The Three Stooges*), a Pathé newsreel, a main feature (usually a comedy) and a cowboy serial.

As the cinema filled up with hordes of children, songs would blast out over the PA system, with the assembled audience joining in more enthusiastically than tunefully. A favourite whose chorus I can still sing went 'Over the mountains, over the sea, that's where my heart is longing to be.' As the auditorium filled up it became a seething mass of little kids, shouting, fighting, climbing over seats.

When the lights dimmed and the curtains swept back to reveal the screen, there was no appreciable reduction in the din made by the packed audience. The commissionairé made heroic efforts to quieten the throng and stop kids throwing popcorn, lollipop sticks and chewing gum at the screen, but without much success. In due course his face would turn the colour of his uniform – maroon. He wasn't called 'Wil Wyllt' (Wild Wil) for nothing.

During the newsreel it was customary for any politicians, of whatever party, to be roundly booed, though I do recall David Morgan speaking up on behalf of Winston Churchill, who had, he told us, 'saved Britain during the war'. We all nodded wisely, giving Winnie the benefit of the doubt, though more in deference to David Morgan, who was two years older than us, than to the wartime prime minister.

The main feature would be greeted on the whole respectfully, with raucous laughter in all the right places. Particularly appreciated was when the Rank Organisation's muscular gongman was relieved of his mallet by Norman Wisdom (cheeky grin, cap with upturned peak), who then gleefully smashed the iconic gong with it.

The episodes of the serial were short, designed only to entice us into the cinema the following Saturday. The quality of the cliffhanger was subject to considerable critical attention. For instance, there was one where the baddie (black hat) had the goodie (white hat) at his mercy on the edge of a cliff. He raised a large rock above his head and ... (the following week) ... raised it too far and fell backwards, to his death. The boos were deafening.

I'll end with a cautionary tale. When I was about eight or nine, it was announced that the price of a ticket for the Saturday matinée was going up from 3d. to 6d. Double! To justify it, the cinema chain said that the price-hike would pay for better-quality, full-colour features. This turned out not to be true. An aspiration, as today's politicians would no doubt have it, rather than a firm commitment. A timely lesson, at an early age, in the shortcomings of business ethics and the ever-presence of corporate greed.

Or would have been, if we'd noticed.

Postscript

Most of the comments on Saturday matinées concerned other films, serials or actors that I failed to mention – *Flash Gordon*, *Tarzan*, Roy Rogers, Dean Martin, Jerry Lewis. Another comment drew attention to the sad plight of those of limited means who lived in outlying villages, for whom a visit to the cinema, matinée or not, was a rare treat. Yet another drew attention to a phenomenon that I'd completely forgotten – the stamping of feet. This would happen when a film was found wanting in excitement or quality, an interval was considered too long, or when the film broke and it was felt that the projectionist was taking too long to repair it.

Taflars

Any weapons we wanted to own, we had to make ourselves. Bows and arrows, spears, even pea-shooters, all had their place. But the most sophisticated, and the most dangerous, were undoubtedly taflars, or catapults. Just because they were made by kids it shouldn't be thought that they were toys.

An English visitor once proudly showed us his metal, shop-bought catapult and, instead of the gasps of admiration he expected, was met only with hoots of derision. Home-made taflars were a source of pride to those who built and owned them.

This is how we made them:

- In the woods we found a suitable Y-shaped branch and cut it to size. Our preference was for ash or sycamore, with their smooth grey or reddish bark. We looked for a sapling which had divided into two equal branches giving a Y-shape with the handle a little thicker than the arms. Least prized was ivy – it was gnarled, rarely straight, and we considered it fit only for novices.

- When we'd freed the basic taflar from its parent tree, we cut a notch around each arm, about an inch below the top.

- We would then take two lengths of square-section elastic (bought from the shop halfway down Penlan Street), fit them into the notch on each arm, and tie them securely. If you couldn't afford the elastic, you could use slashed rubber from the inner tube of a bike, but this was far from ideal.

- We would then pass the other ends of the elastic through holes in a leather (preferably) or canvas (if necessary) patch, and tie securely.

- It remained to proceed to the nearest crab-apple tree (there was a good one on the Garn above Penlleiniau School) to collect ammunition.

- Finally we would gather behind the Garn near Fort Pit (a group of boulders on the summit of a small hill) and choose sides – one group to defend the fort, the other to attack.

- At a signal, defenders would take up their positions, attackers would disperse, and battle would commence.

Notes:

1. As you might gather from the above, the least sought-after taflar was one made of ivy, with inner-tube elastic and a canvas patch.

2. Taflars were formidable weapons, which is why crab apples were used as ammunition. Stones could have killed.

3. Taflars were far superior to all those modern computer combat games. But a lot more painful if you got cornered by one of the big boys.

4. A member of the group commented that she and her grandmother when out walking, had once got caught in the crossfire. She understood the attraction of the game, though, comparing it to paintballing.

Rubbish

Unlikely though it may seem, Pwllheli's council rubbish tip was inspirational for us kids when trying to keep ourselves occupied during the long summer holidays.

- It would be decided, for example (and I don't know how) that it was time to build a go-kart. So we'd scour the tip for two sets of pram wheels, preferably with their axles intact, ideally with one pair smaller than the other. Once found, it was relatively easy to unearth the bits of wood needed for the rest of the construction – a square piece for the seat, a long plank for the chassis, and a shorter plank for the front wheel steering unit. A few nails (and, ideally, a large galvanised staple), a length of rope, and the cart was ready for its test drive. No engine, of course – a slope, a push from your mates, and gravity did the rest. Sometimes it was exhilarating, sometimes it was terrifying, but whatever happened there was a satisfying sense of achievement.

- More difficult (we only ever did it once) was building a bike from parts we found on the tip. When we'd finished it was like Frankenstein's monster – it was never going to win any beauty contests – but also like the monster, it worked. Comfort was minimal – no saddle and no tyres. And when we'd finished, we just returned it to the tip – we all had far better bikes of our own. But again, there was that sense of achievement.

- Finally, and in our opinion most successfully, we built a raft from a big old door and four huge oil drums. We lashed the drums to the door, and it really looked the part. We launched it from Pont Solomon (I have no idea how we got it there) and with one of us on board using a plank of wood as a paddle and the rest of us wading next to it, made our way downriver and out into the inner harbour. And though it really did look the part, it rode far too high in the water and was extremely unstable – whenever we thought we'd cracked it, and got everybody on board, somebody would move, and we'd all be tipped, screaming with laughter, into the water.

These were all, as I said, summer activities. A further one was, of its nature, only possible in winter. We built sledges

– wooden seat and wooden runners lined with the strips of metal from tea chests and packing cases.

Not that we got much chance to use them. Whatever happened in the rest of the UK, we never got much snow in Pwllheli – we seemed to be surrounded by some sort of mild microclimate. Even when it did snow, it was so thin and watery that, by the time we'd built our sledges, the snow had melted.

The only time I got to ride – on a slope somewhere on the Garn – a sledge that I'd built, it ended in humiliation. At the bottom of the slope was a wire fence, which I didn't think there was the slightest chance that I'd reach. I did reach it, and at speed. My sledge shot under the fence and carried on into the distance, leaving me spreadeagled on the wire like Wile E. Coyote.

I was proud of my sledge's performance, and I got off without injury. The only damage I suffered was to my dignity.

Postscript

A number of comments added to this post filled in some details:

- The tip was behind a group of houses called 'Riverside' on the road to Abersoch. This was just after it split from the road to Nefyn at the end of Ala Road, west of the town. You couldn't miss it – you heard the screeches of the seagulls wheeling above it long before you got to the tip itself.

- Apart from shooting rats (I'll come to that later) or scavenging the tip for stuff to make go-karts or bikes or rafts, there was a lot of fun to be had just looking for things, like rude magazines or old film stock dumped by the town's cinemas. This last, when set alight, gave off the most horrendous stink which made your stomach churn and your eyes water. It could even have been poisonous, but we still seem to be around. Or at least I am.

- My memories of building and test driving go-karts led to

further reminiscences. Not just memories, either – one such test drive down the steep hill where Caernarfon Road ran into Sand Street left one member of the group with a permanent reminder – a scar on his foot and a dent in his skull. And you didn't even need a go-kart: just a flattened cardboard box and the summer-dried grass slope above Penlleiniau for deathdefying hurtles which could easily have ended up on the school roof.

Pwllheli Carnival

Pwllheli Carnival must have been an annual event and, according to Google, still is. But the only one in which I took part can be dated precisely to 1953.

I and David and Steven Morgan (more of whom later) went as 'The Conquerors of Everest'. Very topical, chosen by our parents. We were dressed in mountaineering clothes, helmets and goggles, though with wellies instead of climbing boots. That was embarrassing enough. But David was Hunt, and Steven was Sherpa Tenzing. Which meant that I was Hillary. A girl's name! I was mortified!

Postscript

This short post led to several interesting comments:

- When my brother mentioned that he had a photo of 'The Conquerors of Everest' taken by our father, one of them (Sir John Hunt, aka David Morgan) asked if he'd post it on Facebook. This my brother duly did.
- Two further comments supplied interesting claims: that Sir John Hunt retired to Terfyn, a house in the woods near the Bron Eifion Hotel just outside Cricieth, and that Sherpa Tenzing's son attended Atlantic College. I could confirm neither of these intriguing suggestions.

Grown-up attitudes to kids

Grown-ups going about their daily business were surprisingly tolerant of children watching them work:

- On the day of the animal market (Mondays) we'd gather at the Mart and sit on the dividing gates watching the farmers driving their animals through into their allocated pens. Sometimes they'd even let us help, shouting at us to block off a particular escape route, or drive the animals in a particular direction. My memory is that the farmers were gentle with the sheep and cattle, brutal with the pigs.

- More disturbing, we'd sit on the lladd-du (slaughterhouse) wall in the Maes and watch the slaughtermen at work. It amazed us how a huge living bullock could, in a matter of minutes, with the bang of a bolt-gun, the whine of a hoist and the slash of a knife, be turned into sides of beef and a pile of intestines and dung. Later, as underage teenage drinkers sitting on sloping harbour walls, we'd find ourselves being regarded by the calm milky eyes of a floating severed sheep's head, bobbing just out of reach. I assume this was the result of the illicit dumping by the slaughterhouse of waste products into the harbour.

- In an alley behind the High Street's Leader Press, we'd watch the printer making types. He'd melt the printer's metal (traditionally an alloy of lead, tin and antimony, so Wikipedia informs me) in a little crucible, then pour the shining liquid into the moulds. When he'd finished and cleared up, we'd find little silver types scattered on the ground, and collect them, trying to spell out (backwards) our own names.

- We'd watch the market traders, shouting at each other in their exotic English or Indian accents, as they set up their stalls in the Maes on Wednesdays, or the men working

33

on the boats in Baines, or the porters and railwaymen doing their jobs at the station.

I'm sure it's still the same, though perhaps in different ways, with different jobs. God bless grown-ups who tolerate, even welcome, kids' interest in their work.

CHAPTER 2

On the Cusp of Adolescence

So FAR, MY memories of growing up in Pwllheli are of being a kid among others, roaming far and wide looking for things to do. As the Bible has it: 'When I was a child I spoke as a child, I understood as a child, I thought as a child.' But with the approach of adolescence, it all became more complex. Some of the things we used to do simply faded away – we put away childish things. But others, in some settings, became adapted to our growing maturity. Christmas activities developed with age. We still risked our lives, but in more adult, though no less foolish, ways. Fear of the police, initially sparked by scrumping apples or shoplifting toys, elided into worry about being done for criminal damage or underage drinking. When we were kids we went on a Sunday school trip to the beach at Llandudno; when we were older, it was to a Beatles gig at Llandudno's Odeon. Butlins remained a garden of delights, but the nature of the delights altered. The frame stayed the same, the picture changed. And, on the cusp between childhood and adolescence, watching our older brothers and sisters, we became dimly aware of the approaching storm.

A sign of things to come

As time went on, we noticed something strange. The older boys, the ones we'd looked up to all our lives, suddenly started to do inexplicable things. They combed their hair. They had baths. They took pride in their clothes – their drapes, their drainpipes, their crepe-soled suede shoes. They drank coffee in the Expresso coffee-bar, fed threepenny bits into the juke box. They hung around Studt's fairground. Why weren't they with us, roaming the Garn or enjoying pitched taflar battles at Fort Pit?

Then it got worse. They went to the pictures with girls. They danced in the Legion Hall. They bought off-licence bottles and drank them beside the harbour or on the beach. They did evening or weekend jobs, or worked in Butlins.

We kids muttered mutinously among ourselves about this total betrayal. We would, we assured each other, never let it happen to us. Why were they doing it?

We would find out.

The search for a base

There was an unwritten agreement between us and our parents that, at weekends and during holidays, we would make ourselves scarce until mealtimes. Fine when it was fine – there were hundreds of places in Pwllheli and the surrounds to keep us occupied. But what about when it was wet? Despite my fond belief that Pwllheli in the mid-twentieth century was bathed in eternal sunshine, I realise on reflection that actually it rained. Quite a lot. So where did we go when it was wet?

Sometimes it was just killing time under cover – looking around the antique shop in John Goddard's under the Town Hall, cruising Woolworths and Peacocks, trying nonchalantly to get a glimpse of naked women on the cover of *Health and Efficiency* on the sloping racks of Wyman's, the station newsagents, window-shopping under the iron-and-glass arcades in Cardiff Road or Station Square, or sitting on top of the tidal gates under the Pen Cob bridge.

But if fortune smiled on you, you had friends with access to far better alternatives. No more meandering half-heartedly in the wet under whatever shelter you could find. Access was granted to premium, gold-standard five-star all-weather accommodation!

David and Steven Morgan's dad was the manager of W.H. Smiths. At the end of an alley next to the shop was the stock room. A kids' Shangri-La – a warehouse full of newspapers and magazines and, especially, comics! We could laze around all day, working our way through the *Beano* and the *Dandy*, the *Topper* and the *Beezer*, the *Eagle*, and lots more. When we were a bit older we'd even sneak a look at girls' comics like *Roxy* or *Jackie*, with their soppy love stories; though, if confronted, would furiously deny it.

Beyond the stockroom was a pear-tree-dotted garden with, at the far end, a stone-built shed, which we used as a sort of 'gang hut'. We could sit around inside and even, on hot summer days, climb through the skylight and lie on the roof, feeling the heat radiating off the slates. I spent a whole afternoon trying (and failing) to interpret the *I-Spy* code book so that I could read Big Chief's secret messages in Dad's *News Chronicle*.

The combination of the stockroom, the garden and the shed provided a wonderful year-round facility for pre-teens like us. As we got older, though, we felt we needed something a bit more sophisticated. This is where Dafydd Bodlew came in. Dafydd was the son of a local vet whose practice occupied the ground floor of a building off Ala Road. Above the practice were two vacant rooms which he allowed his son to use. So it became an unofficial early-teen youth club.

A lot of the detail has faded with time – I wish I had photos. We sat in comfortable chairs, we could smoke without adult interference, I think we had tea, coffee and soft drinks. There was a pen bearing a picture of a woman in a black bathing costume – when you held it upside down, her bathing costume would slowly drain away, leaving her naked!

The thing we most valued, however, was an ancient wind-up gramophone, which came with an equally ancient collection of records. It didn't take us long to get sick of the few big shellac discs though (there was a limit to how much David Whitfield we could take), so we agreed to contribute part of our pocket money (6*d.*, I think) each month to a record fund. We wanted to listen to something more modern. Our first purchase was 'Summertime Blues' by Eddie Cochran. We didn't know much about music, but what an absolute classic to start our collection! One of our number (Merfyn, or Myfs, from Caeau Brychion farm) played it continuously for a whole weekend. He got through a full packet of needles. And still we loved it!

Then, at first imperceptibly then totally, W.H. Smiths and the Ala Road vets were replaced by the new kid on the block – a café which became teen-headquarters for much of the youth of Pwllheli.

Enter the Expresso Coffee Bar, or 'Brexo'.

Christmas

My earliest memories of Christmas are from the late 1940s and first half of the 1950s, when I was little.

I knew the great day was approaching when at school we made calendars and rehearsed for the nativity play, and at home Mum and Dad prepared for us to move into the front room, used during the rest of the year only for visitors. The fire was lit, the decorations were hung, the tree was collected, put in place and trimmed (including real candles attached to the branches with little tin clamps – were they insane?), and the dust was blown off the bottle of sherry in preparation for the vicar's Christmas day visit. My brothers and I bought presents for Dad (always golf-related, progressing from tees to the more expensive golf balls) and Mum. My brother Jeff and I, one year, pooled our money to buy her a tin-opener, and couldn't understand the coolness with which it was received.

Above all, we wrote our own present lists, then set fire to them in the kitchen grate to watch them float up the chimney, on their way to the North Pole. Did we believe all this malarkey? Of course not. Rather, like my grandchildren in more recent times, we refused to admit to any doubts in case they resulted in Father Christmas, and more importantly the presents, disappearing for ever.

On Christmas Eve we'd ceremonially hang our stockings from the mantelpiece, complaining that you couldn't get many presents into a stocking. This was an annual pantomime – we knew that by next morning the stockings would have been replaced by pillowcases.

Then it was up to bed.

What followed was in some ways a nightmare. Feverish excitement, desperately trying to get to sleep so that tomorrow could come, and finally dropping off, completely exhausted, at four in the morning.

After an hour's sleep, it remained to thunder down to the front room ('Father Christmas has been!') for a morning of tearing wrapping paper off presents, stuffing ourselves with chocolate and, before going to church, being forced to eat porridge which would lie like cement in our stomachs for the rest of the day. On the way to church, town looked like it did on a Sunday – empty – except for the kids doing test runs with their new bikes or scooters or roller skates or dolls' prams.

I have no memory of the Christmases of my early teens. I think they must have been more muted than the ecstasies of my childhood, but with the pleasure of seeing a younger brother – Chris – enjoying the day the way I had ten years before. As I was now a teenager, though, this would have been overlaid with a veneer of adolescent scepticism. You couldn't get too excited if you wanted to be cool.

Things changed as soon as I went away to university.

When at home for the holiday I was no longer expected to spend Christmas Eve with the family. Christmas now meant meeting friends, catching up after three months away, and consuming an inordinate amount of alcohol. Hello adulthood, and a welcome template for years to come. But there was that sneaking feeling that something had been lost.

Then I got married and had kids and, hey, the golden Christmases were back! When they in turn started to fade, grandchildren came along, and off we went again.

Although seventy years separates my remembered childhood Christmases from those being enjoyed now by my youngest grandchild, the traditions of decorating the tree, buying and wrapping the presents (though we now put them under the tree rather than in stockings or pillowcases), getting up in the dark – the anticipation and excitement are all exactly the same. Even the carols haven't changed. The once in the year when the whole family could get together.

Until Covid, of course.

Postscript

As might be expected, my post on Christmas led to a burst of memories from other members of the group, some of which really made me laugh:

- My younger brother Chris commented that he too had bought our mother a tin opener for Christmas, but this time she'd actually asked for one. Our father gave him ten shillings to buy the present, and he trotted down to Woolworths where he discovered that a tin opener only cost five. What should he do? His solution was simple. He bought her two.

- At what age did we stop believing in Father Christmas? I think the latest admitted to was twelve. It may be, of course, that there are some in the Facebook group who *still* believe. To those, I offer my sincere apologies. I should have posted a spoiler alert.

- It was touching the lengths to which fathers would go to bring a bit of extra magic to their kids' Christmases. One girl who lived on a farm noticed that Santa would wait till her father had gone to milk the cows, then appear at the window and wave to her. When her dad came back in from milking, he'd remark that he'd just met Father Christmas out in the farmyard. She only began to suspect the truth when she found Santa's suit in the cowshed.

- Another father, a senior member of YRP's teaching staff, would, on Christmas Eve, claim that he had books to mark. After going into another room, a ghostly voice would emanate from the fireplace ('Oes 'na blant da yna?' 'Are there good children there?'). Screeching and giggling at this manifestation of 'Siôn Corn', his kids would rush into the next room to find their father marking his books, calmly, if a little out of breath. Much later, he admitted that he'd discovered a vent in the chimney.

- My grandson said, out of the blue, that he didn't believe in Father Christmas. His voice was derisive. 'Nobody could deliver all those presents to all the children in the world in one night.' 'Who delivers them then?' I asked. He looked smug. 'The Easter Bunny!'

I don't like Sundays

My memory tells me that, on Sundays in Pwllheli, everything was shut – shops, cafés, pubs, restaurants, cinemas. Bus services were severely curtailed, and there were hardly any cars on the road. Tumbleweed blew down the High Street, turned left at the Whitehall, and continued down Gaol Street to the Maes.

To make matters worse, I never went out with friends on a Sunday, and TV (we only had one channel) was even worse on the Sabbath than it was for the rest of the week.

I realise now that these memories are probably inaccurate. Bodawen Café *was* open on Sundays. Restricted services on buses couldn't have affected me – I never needed to catch a bus. And when I was old enough to drink, there was always the Conservative Club, where people I knew were willing to sign me in.

OK, I admit. I invented the tumbleweed for comic effect.

The only places that seemed to be open were the churches and chapels. To others these establishments may have been a source of spiritual nurturing and quiet contemplation. But to me, they were instrumental in generating the gloom that hung over Pwllheli's Sundays like a thundercloud. Or specifically, one of them was – come on down, St Peter's Church.

I had to go to church three times on Sunday – morning (English), afternoon (Sunday school) and evening (Welsh). Three to four hours, and deadly dull. For us choirboys the routines were set in stone – arrive at the vestry, change into cassock and surplice, go out into the nave to put up the hymn numbers, wait for the bell to stop, lead the choir (carrying a cross) around the church, then take a seat in the choir stalls – boys in the front row, men in the second. Absolute tedium – if God did exist, we thought, why did he put us through all this, why didn't he take pity on us?

Diversions to alleviate the boredom were few and far between – very slim pickings indeed. I can recall only a handful:

- Before the service, a quick fag and a laugh with fellow choristers in the Tower Hotel yard, across the road to the church.

- Huw Pierce-Jones's first sermon after his arrival as vicar, having a pop at Salem chapel, just down the road.

- The occasional visiting hellfire preacher who horrified our gentle Anglican congregation with drama, histrionics and damnation.

- English summer visitors with their (sometimes) pretty daughters.

- The singing of favourite hymns. Mine was 'For those in

peril on the sea.' The opening – 'Eternal father, strong to save' – still sends shivers up and down my spine.

- The first Easter with a new and enthusiastic vicar, when he instructed everybody in the congregation to turn to the person to their right, shake hands, and say, 'Heddwch' (Peace). The adults didn't know where to look, and the kids desperately tried not to laugh.

- My brother at his wedding, kneeling next to his bride at the front of the church, with the price-tag of his new shoes there for all to see.

- Of all the diversions that helped to save our sanity, though, the most spectacular was when a lightbulb, dropping down from the circular fitting high above the choir, smashed onto the bald head of Mr Roberts (father of Robert, John, Wil, Katrin Ellen and Benny). Mr Roberts totally ignored this assault, as did, following his lead, the rest of the congregation. Even we choirboys who were notorious gigglers kept a straight face. The humans behaved with dignity, God not so much.

To this day, even though shops and pubs are open everywhere and on TV there are 'fifty-seven channels and nothin' on', a feeling of depression and ennui creeps over me on Sundays. There are those, I know, who pine for the peace and quiet of the traditional Sabbath.

Not me. I'm always glad to get it over with.

Postscript

My dislike of Pwllheli Sundays led to a storm of fellow-feeling:

- Television's *Big Match* came in for a kicking, partly by being on when kids had to go to Sunday school, but also for being heavily biased towards teams from the south of England. A Manchester City supporter's imagined link says it all. Brian Moore: 'Today we show a goalless game

43

from second division Craven Cottage and follow it with an eight-goal thriller from Maine Road...'

- The hypocrisy of non-churchgoing parents forcing their reluctant children to go to church, especially on sunny summer days when they'd far rather be at the beach, was a source of bitter resentment.

- The fact that Pwllheli was 'dry' on Sundays earned a mention, with two of the clubs at which locals could get a Sunday pint being saluted as welcome retreats from teetotalism. Though, at the Legion, Twm Spanners came in for some stick for his choice of acts for the cabaret, and it was observed that many members of the Conservative Club (even, whisper it, members of the committee) were actually supporters of Plaid Cymru. Some drinkers at the Con Club also took a dim view of the portraits of ex-Tory Prime Ministers looking disapprovingly down on their tippling from the walls.

- It was observed that morning services in one church were lengthy and leisurely, whilst evening services were taken at a fair lick, with the vicar rattling through the prayerbook and knocking back the leftover Communion wine at a rate of knots. It was speculated that he wanted to get home for a favourite TV programme. No video recording then, of course.

- Finally, a couple of people said that Sundays in Pwllheli had put them off religion for life. Being told that they would burn in hell didn't go down at all well: 'God was on borrowed time,' said one, and another, 'It was the secular life for me.'

Risking it

It's true that Pwllheli and the area around was a wonderful adventure playground for us local kids, but with the benefit of hindsight I have to admit that we did some really – I mean *really* – stupid things, stuff that we were lucky to survive. For example:

- We used to climb around on Llanbedrog headland looking for seagulls' eggs. For no good reason – we didn't eat them, we didn't collect them. We'd edge along, clinging to tufts of rough grass, being attacked by furious seabirds, with terrifying drops beneath us to the jagged rocks and surging breakers below.

- On stormy days we'd jump across 'crochan berw' (boiling cauldron), a great split in Gimblet Rock. Seas barrelled in below us; then, as the waves crashed into the rock face, they'd shoot into the air, creating forty-foot columns of foam and spray which climbed above us, paused, then roared back down, soaking us all.

- We'd bounce along the inspection gangway under the bridge at the town end of the Cob to sit on top of the huge tidal gates. If the tide was out, there was a big drop down to the rushing shallows; if the tide was in, it felt a lot safer with the water just a couple of feet below, but the boiling eddies and undertows told a different story.

- Pushing through the fence a couple of hundred yards from the railway station, we'd place pennies (and these were old pennies – big and thick) on the line, lie down on the gravel beside the track to wait for the train to pass, then collect the resulting metal discs, now huge and blade-thin.

- Playing tick/hide-and-seek on the Garn after dark, wielding huge chrome Pifco four-cell torches. It was like a light-sabre battle, or the introduction to 20th Century Fox films.

These were regular childhood occurrences. In adolescence, I would have to own up to a couple of drink-related one-offs:

- Walking back to Pwllheli after an evening at the Glyn-y-Weddw, we were crossing Carreg-y-Defaid headland.

Garnett, behind me, turned to the rest of the boys and said, 'Follow Jos, he knows the way.' If only this were true. When he turned back I'd disappeared. I'd fallen off a cliff. It wasn't the path I thought it was. Luckily, the cliff wasn't very high, I missed the rocks at the bottom, and I survived.

- Coming back from a dance in Nefyn in Dick Tudweiliog's VW Beetle, we took that kink in the road around the shop in Efailnewydd too fast, ending up with the car screeching along on its roof. When the car had rocked to a standstill, upside down, there was an eerie silence, broken eventually when I said, 'Oops!' Brave or what? As Martin Amis said of himself in a similar situation, 'brave as a lord, brave as a newt'. With the help of villagers who'd ventured out with hurricane lamps, we bounced the car back onto its wheels, climbed back in through the space where the rear window had been, and continued on our draughty way, all of us crouching low because the roof had dropped by several feet.

Thinking about all this, fifty to sixty years later, my blood runs cold. How could I have been so stupid as to threaten not only my own existence, but that of my eventual two children and three grandchildren? Though in my own defence, I didn't know about them at the time.

God's creatures

It has surprised me how many of my childhood memories have involved animals, and not in a good way. As far as God's creatures are concerned, my mates and I have little reason to be proud.

I've already mentioned in previous posts that we watched cattle, sheep and pigs being killed in the slaughterhouse on the Maes, that we helped farmers, often with considerable brutality, direct their stock in the Mart, that we collected

46

seagulls' eggs on Llanbedrog headland, just for the hell of it. Additional memories today make me uncomfortable:

- Shooting rats on the council tip at the end of Ala Road with Ian Martin's air rifle. Not in the interests of vermin control, but just for fun.

- Catching crabs in the harbour (no lewd comments, please – we were kids), impaling them on our pocket knives, then tossing their corpses onto the pile that had been growing all summer on the buttress separating the huge tidal gates.

- Carrying slow worms around in our pockets and using them to frighten girls. I never owned one myself, but I did look after Steven Morgan's whilst he was away.

- Capturing crow chicks, hoping to raise them as pets. When I tried it, my father, saying it was cruel, made me set it free in the garden. Within seconds our cat had killed it.

- Throwing flat, sharp stones hard into the huge jellyfish that sometimes got stranded on the beach or on the edges of the harbour. You could see the track made by the stone as it sliced through the jellyfish's flesh.

- Killing rabbits on the Garn by dropping rocks on them. This was OK, we told ourselves – they were dying of myxomatosis and we were just putting them out of their misery. But there's no doubting the relish with which we watched their eyes glaze over and blood spurt from their mouths.

- Trailing mackerel lines as we made our way back from Butlins on one of Dick Parry's boats. We used silver paper as bait to catch the first, then slivers of the silvery underside of the first to catch the rest. Common practice, I think, but on reflection, a bit macabre. Though this is offset by the fact that at least we ate the mackerel.

- Garnett Morris on Gimblet Rock, using Brian Kerr's

Webley air pistol to pretend to be a gunslinger. He drew the gun and, in one smooth movement, took a pot-shot at a tiny bird flitting high above us. The bird dropped like a stone, dead. 'Great shot,' we shouted, then seeing his face, 'Million-to-one chance – it wasn't your fault.' This story actually reflects well on Garnett. Not so much on the rest of us.

- My last story doesn't really fit this sorry tale of pointless cruelty but is far too good to leave out. In the Sailing Club one night a man asked me if I wanted to buy a salmon. He led me out to his car. Three large fish took up, with the back seats down, its whole length – I had no idea that salmon were so big. 'Aren't you afraid that the gamekeeper'll catch you?' I asked. He grinned. 'I *am* the gamekeeper!'

Visits to the dentist

Visits to the dentist are not really the stuff of nostalgia. But I've got a couple of memories that could almost claim to be – well – nostalgic.

First up – a trip to the school dentist. One day, several of us at Penlleiniau were called out after prayers and told to walk down Salem Terrace and Gaol Street and up past the station to the Legion Hall. We were to be unaccompanied. We loved the independence and the break from routine. When we got to the Legion we were put in a little office opposite the entrance, where we chatted, played word games and generally messed about. Again, no adult supervision.

That was the good bit.

Then, one by one, the nurse called out our names. I was the first to go. In the centre of the hall was a circle of medical screens within which stood the dentist's chair, dwarfed by a Heath Robinson contraption made up of steel rods, cords and pulleys with a foot-treadle at the base. In its shadow stood the dentist himself.

That day I had two fillings and an extraction. The drilling – a slow and painful grind with the dentist's foot pumping the treadle and the machine rattling and swaying above my open mouth – was followed by a quick packing in of the amalgam. For the extraction, the needle was plunged into my gum and the tooth yanked out – immediately, without waiting for the anaesthetic to take effect.

That was the bad bit.

A quick swill of pink water, and I was back in the waiting room. When we'd all been done, we set off back to school. On the way, my mouth, far too late, froze, and I bit my cheek whilst having dinner, but only found out when the anaesthetic wore off. In trying to drink water from the beaker it slurped out of the spongy side of my mouth and, embarrassingly, down the front of my trousers.

My second memory was of a visit to Cowell's surgery at the bottom of Salem Terrace. I must have been fifteen or sixteen. After a sleepless night of excruciating toothache, he'd diagnosed an abscess, and said that the tooth would have to come out. But he couldn't do it immediately – it would involve a general anaesthetic, and he therefore needed to arrange the presence of a doctor. He sent me home for another sleepless night, munching aspirins like sweets. By the time I returned the next morning, my face was so swollen that it was twisted grotesquely, as if my mouth was trying to bite my left earlobe. 'No doubt about my diagnosis,' he said cheerfully. I was put under with gas and he whipped out the tooth.

After the extraction, I went home and slept for the rest of the day. When I came to, I checked the swelling. It was even worse – I looked like Quasimodo!

With a scarf wrapped around my head, I went to the Liberal Club, a snooker hall just off Penlan Street, where we often used to hang out. Michael Bowie asked what the scarf was for. I explained. He persuaded me to take it off, agreeing to my stipulation that he mustn't, under any circumstances, laugh. I unwound the scarf.

49

To his credit, he did his very best. But eventually he couldn't hold it in any longer. The dam burst and he doubled up. I quickly became the focus of a circle of snooker players, and even some of the old men playing billiards on the half-size tables. All were holding both their cues and their sides.

I couldn't help joining in, painful though it was.

'Does it hurt?' goes the old joke. 'Only when I laugh.'

The police

Watching a documentary called *The Pembrokeshire Murders* on TV started me thinking about the police and my memories of them in Pwllheli. No doubt they, like police anywhere, had to deal with murders, domestic violence, fights, burglaries and all the other staples of TV cop shows. Inevitably, though, what I remember was the less glamorous side of policing, as seen through the eyes of a child and then an adolescent.

Whether it was scrumping apples, ringing doorbells and running away or sneaking into the Palladium through emergency doors opened by a mate, each crime was followed by days of abject dread that the police would pay a visit. After one such crime (shoplifting toys from Woolworths) I nearly wet myself when, answering a knock on our front door, I saw, through one of its frosted glass panels, the unmistakeable dome-topped shape of a policeman. In sombre tones he said that he wanted to see my father, and they withdrew into the front room. Muttering promises to God that I would henceforth live a totally blameless life, I was on the verge of pleading guilty and holding my wrists out for the handcuffs when they came out. The policeman cheerily ruffled my hair, turned to Dad and said, 'Goodnight Mr Simon,' and went on his way. There had apparently been a break-in at Dad's school. My vow to God was quickly forgotten.

The worst offence we were involved in happened in early adolescence. We'd decided (as you do) that we'd see if we could get us all onto the roof of some lock-up garages behind the

Palladium within a certain time limit. With one remaining person to go, and five seconds before the deadline, someone shouted, 'One last heave!' and there was a loud crack. The corrugated asbestos roof gave way, and we were deposited into the garage. We didn't have to discuss what to do – without a word, we swarmed up the broken sheet of roofing that leaned against the wall, dropped down outside, and hared off in all directions. We spent the next week wretchedly waiting for the heavy knock on our front doors. But it never came, and we thanked our lucky stars that there hadn't been a Lamborghini or Ferrari in the garage at the time. Had there been, we suspected the investigation would have been far more thorough.

As we got into our mid-teens, most of our police-related worries were to do with under-age drinking. In Llanbedrog, it was rumoured that the local bobbie had a routine. He'd check the Ship at the top of the village for under-eighteens, then walk down to the Glyn-y-Weddw to do the same there. Whether he had a crafty pint at either or both, I've no idea. Based on this routine, the recommended procedure for under-age drinkers was to start in the Glyn-y-Weddw, then, at about eight o'clock, walk up the hill to the Ship, often greeting, with a cheery goodnight, the policeman who was walking in the opposite direction.

In Cricieth, on Memorial Hall dance nights, the town was flooded with a build-up of teens and early twenties, increasingly the worse for wear. In response, the police presence grew as the night progressed. The relatively sedate early evening – before the influx of the forces of law and order – we'd spend at The Railway, or sometimes the Brynhir. But nearer the last-entry Memorial Hall cut-off point, we'd stop for a final pint at the Prince of Wales. It was directly across the road to the dancehall, and more importantly, the bar had two entrances – one on the High Street, the other on the road down to the beach. So, if a police raid took place, whichever door they came through, we could drift nonchalantly but swiftly out through the other.

On reflection, then, although the police were ever-present in the nightmares of my youth, my actual experience of them was minimal – in fact, my only direct interaction with the long arm of the law was when reporting the theft of my bike (which, the next day, I discovered that I'd actually left outside the Liberal Club). Indeed, my main attitude to the police was one of sympathy: for the lonely PC patrolling inside the Memorial Hall as gangs of youths gave each other hard looks as preludes to fights, or the young constable who, shortly after being posted to Pwllheli, had his bike thrown into the harbour.

The only policeman I knew by name was Inspector Shaw, who was in charge of the whole of Llŷn. I don't think I ever met him, though after his retirement he might have served me a pint in his Tudweiliog pub.

Postscript

Comments about the police in Pwllheli were generally positive, and even amusing:

- The son of a past coxswain of Pwllheli Lifeboat reports that his dad often got calls in the small hours from the police worried about a flashing light out at sea. His response was to ask if any rookies had joined the local force recently. If the answer was yes, he would ask that they time the flashes, and if they were seventeen seconds apart, be assured that it was the St Tudwal's lighthouse.

- Local people noticed that big influxes of police officers seemed to coincide with visits to the harbour by Irish trawlers. Since this was during 'The Troubles' in Ireland, they drew their own conclusions.

- My brother tells me that a policeman called at our house to confer with our father about alleged shoplifting by some Penlleiniau pupils. Having left the house, he returned in search of his pipe and tobacco, only to find that, when he removed his helmet as he entered the house, he'd put them into it for safe keeping.

- There was a diverting story of skulduggery involving the mistaken identity of a policeman's bike. I think I got the gist of it – it was in Welsh, and when I tried to check my inexpert interpretation by clicking on 'translation', it really wasn't much help.

- There was a long thread of stories involving the police in Germany which, though hilarious, are not really appropriate here, though should surely see the light of day in some other future publication.

- Several people noted that kids in north Wales were generally afraid of the police, and that, in view of the present-day decline in respect for authority figures, this was perhaps no bad thing.

- We also heard from somebody who had been a young copper in Pwllheli in the early 1980s, and who had developed such an abiding love of the area that he has visited Llŷn on holiday ever since. He asked to share the post with other officers who'd served in Pwllheli, so they must still stay in touch.

The beach

If you were a kid in Pwllheli, the beach was an ever-present part of your life. In fact, not 'beach', but 'beaches' – we were blessed with three:

- Abererch Beach, which boasted fine, almost white, sand, impressive dunes, excellent for playing hide-and-seek or digging tunnels, and water that seemed always to be warm. This last was perhaps because it was shallow, which also made Abererch Beach a favourite with families with young children. A shack of a café, up to its armpits in drifted sand, offered refreshments.

- South Beach was closer to town and at different times sandy and pebbly, with a seabed that shelved downwards so steeply that, diving in, you'd be out of your depth in seconds. The nearby Beach Café had a shop selling the usual seaside stuff – buckets, spades, lilos, fishing nets, snorkels, masks, flippers – with, beyond it, a sit-down café. Next to it stood public toilets – handy if you didn't intend to swim, and therefore couldn't pee in the sea.

- West End was similar to South Beach, but with Marram grass and sea holly. There were two shops nearby – one next to the Caelloi coach garage, the other on the way to the Rec.

South Beach and West End were the most popular because they were close to the town centre and easily accessible on foot or by bike. You could always tell when kids were on their way to the beach. They'd have trunks rolled up in a towel tucked under the tool kit hanging from the back of their bike saddles. More serious swimmers carried flippers, snorkel and mask slung in carrier bags under the handlebars.

I don't think we realised at the time how lucky we were. Leaning our bikes against the prom wall, we'd get changed (with all sorts of comical under-towel gymnastics to preserve our modesty) and head for the sea. There were those hardy souls who'd simply sprint down to the water's edge and dive in, and others, more wimpish, who'd take their time. I was a time-taker. Gingerly wading into the water, I was so slow that by the time I was fully immersed, the rest of the boys would have splashed around to their heart's content, walked dripping up the beach, dressed, grown up, got married and had kids. Yes, it took me that long.

After swimming, we'd lie on our towels, build sandcastles, play French cricket, collect shells, smoke. On the beach the sounds – of kids shouting, dogs barking, waves flopping onto the sand, tinny music blaring from (recently invented) transistor radios – seemed oddly muted. It was almost peaceful.

I can picture it now. To the east, Gimblet Rock, to the west, Carreg-y-Defaid, Llanbedrog headland and the St Tudwal's Islands, all shimmering in the heat. Out in the bay, a huge steel tripod, built as a target for trainee bombers from RAF Penrhos. The horizon, dotted with yachts, spinnakers billowing. A raft anchored offshore, for kids to swim to and dive off.

As we got into our teens, the sand would sometimes be abandoned in favour of the rocks – Gimblet to the east, Carreg-y-Defaid to the west. Strong-swimming extraverts of both sexes would dive or jump, screeching, off the rocks into the sea. Weak-swimming introverts like me could only look on with pretended indifference, secretly boiling with admiration and envy.

Since growing up and leaving Pwllheli, certain questions have occurred to me. Why didn't we do our under-age drinking on the beach? We did it in dilapidated shelters on the prom that often smelled of pee, but never more pleasantly sitting on the sand. Why didn't we have barbecues? We'd seen Sandra Dee enjoying lū'aus in *Gidget* and *A Summer Place*. Why didn't we have them in Pwllheli? Too cold? No money? Local byelaws? I can't help feeling that, although as kids we enjoyed our beaches to the full, as teenagers we missed a trick. Or perhaps everybody else *did* have barbecues on the beach, and it was just that I wasn't invited.

For most of my life I haven't been much of a beach person. Bright sunlight gives me a headache, and sand gets into all sorts of places where it really isn't welcome. Don't get me wrong, I still have a lot of time for beaches, but only when I'm sitting above them on a bar terrace, in a comfortable chair, under a parasol, with an ice-cold lager at my elbow and a book open on my lap.

Could it be that beaches are better recollected than experienced?

Or is it just that I've become an archetypal grumpy old man.

Postscript

It was clear from the comments that it wasn't just Pwllheli kids who were blessed with beaches to die for:

- Trefor was a children's idyll of swimming from boat to boat, of diving and crabbing, of petrol-painted rainbows on the water's surface and starfish far below on the seabed.

- Llanbedrog's sheltered beach had floats, canoes and rowing boats for hire and, to the delight of local youths, a constant supply of English girls to chat up from The Warren caravan site. The headland was great for getting away from the crowds that thronged the beach, and for avoiding the police when they became aware of the underage drinking that went on, and for building fires on which to cook sausages and baked potatoes, and around which to drink beer from Party Fours and Party Sevens. When life got a bit repetitive in Llanbedrog, there were always the bright lights of Pwllheli and Abersoch within walking distance in either direction.

And on Pwllheli's beaches, adult entrepreneurship was much in evidence.

- The man who sold pop and lager from a cool box in the back of his estate car. On Sundays the lager was particularly popular with visitors – pubs were closed in Dwyfor (though locals could, of course, drink in one of the numerous clubs in town).

- Again, it was recounted by a neighbour that the lady who'd set up the café on Abererch Beach had first arrived in Pwllheli from Liverpool to work as a waitress, had married a local man, and settled in the area. During the summer she would rise at dawn to bake cakes and scones to be sold in the café that day, whilst in the evening her husband would bring home, in an old biscuit tin, the cash he'd collected in car parking fees. Her business acumen was well rewarded – her house was, apparently, much admired.

Butlins

Butlins Camp, four miles east of the town, dominated the lives of people in Pwllheli in the 1950s and '60s. The camp, when full, was after all two-and-a-half times bigger than the town (ten thousand to four thousand), and Pwllheli was flooded with campers throughout the summer, especially on Wednesdays, when the market took over the Maes.

For us kids, Butlins was a great place to go for the day. First of all there were not one, but two swimming pools – outdoor, next to the main Pwllheli to Cricieth road, with fountains at either end, and indoor, in a building in South Camp, with voyeur-friendly windows giving an underwater view of the thrashing limbs of the swimmers. Both pools were heated, though in the outdoor one it was hard to tell. Then there was the boating lake, on the left just over the bridge into South Camp. It had proper rowing boats, as well as little metal tubs with handles that drove paddles on either side. The rowing boats were great unless the oars slipped out of the rowlocks, in which case you ended up on your back in the bows. The paddleboats were fun until you started to get blisters. We loved thrashing between the islands, setting the ducks quacking in alarm.

During the day, on the open space between North and South Camps, there would be various children's activities run by the redcoats, and for adults, more sophisticated diversions like 'knobbly knees' and 'glamorous grandmother' competitions. Lunchtime announcements over the camp loudspeakers would summon campers to their dining-room sittings. The big ballrooms would be open during the day, and people would sit around in them talking whilst the kids chased each other around or skidded across the empty dancefloor. For staff, these were good places to eat sandwiches if it was wet.

In the evenings there were shows, though I never had much time for them. Next to the stage a screen would occasionally come to life with a message, 'Baby crying in chalet C24' and such. Imagine leaving your baby alone, depending on the 'chalet patrol' to alert you if it woke up!

Although all the entertainment in Butlins was free, entrance to the camp wasn't – so you had to use one of two secret access routes. One, next to a rarely-used vehicle gate on the main road opposite a chapel, had the great advantage of being easy, and getting you right into the heart of North Camp. The disadvantage, though, was that it was visible from the security block at the main gate. Furthermore, anybody passing, on the road or in the camp, could see you. Using it involved flattening yourself against a nearby wall, waiting until the coast was clear, then doing a sprint and a scramble over the fence. It was just like escapes from Nazi POW camps in the war films we loved. Except that we were trying to break in, not out. And there were no searchlights. Or attack dogs. Or armed guards. Or machine-gun towers. Oh alright, it was nothing like escapes from Nazi POW camps.

The other illicit access route involved a long looping trudge across farmer's fields down towards the beach giving an approach from the south, the soft underbelly of Butlins security. It was on a night-time stumble across this field, after a convivial evening in the Pig and Whistle, that I discovered that, yes, horses can sleep standing up. I walked into one.

Apart from all the free entertainment, Butlins was also, for many of us, our first experience of paid employment. And when you worked for Butlins, you didn't have to worry about getting in – your staff pass would do the trick. My first taste was a Saturday job carrying luggage. You were given an ID card and a trolley to carry the cases (this was in the days before suitcases had their own wheels). You didn't actually get paid – Billy Butlin wasn't known for his generosity to his workers. But we didn't think of it as child exploitation – the tips were good. You could make up to a fiver in a day – not bad money for the time. The best tippers were gangs of lads who came in by train. They'd pile their bags onto your trolley, walk up the long road to East Camp in the highest of spirits, then empty their pockets of change into your cupped hands without even counting it. Although the families who came into South Camp weren't so generous, you could get far more trips in because the car park was close to the chalets, so it evened things out.

My last Butlins job was working on Dick Parry's boats, taking trips out into the bay from the beach, which I did for two seasons. During the first, I decided to teach myself to rollerskate. So, each lunchtime, I caught the chairlift to the camp rink from the beach. I didn't do too badly to begin with – I could skate in a straight line reasonably competently. I would plod away until I hit the fence, then reposition whilst hanging on – I never did learn to turn. Think of a new-born giraffe trying to stand up. It finally took a tiny child skating between my legs, then contemptuously laughing as he sped off, backwards, to make me decide that my dignity could stand it no longer, and I jacked it in.

In between my first Butlins job as a Saturday trolley-boy, and my last working for Dick Parry on the boats, I got, courtesy of a member of Butlins Camp's management (my friend Jonesy's dad), a proper, full-time summer job for Butlins, with a weekly wage packet. This involved being:

- A porter in the big camp department store in, I think, the Gaiety Building. They'd over-recruited, so I had very little to do. Mrs Roberts, the manageress, though a bit of a tartar, was sympathetic, and would turn a blind eye to my gradually expanding tea breaks. Most of the girls serving behind the counters were English, so there was some fun to be had in offering scurrilously inappropriate Welsh translations when they asked how to tell their Welsh boyfriends that they loved them. I hope it didn't get them into trouble.

- In charge of the staff coffee bar. A plum job, this. Free coffee, tea and snacks all day, and, courtesy of the key to the jukebox, an infinite choice of music.

- Night work waiting on tables in the Viennese Bar. I did this only once, before deciding that it wasn't for me. Such was my pleasure in spending time in bars, that I didn't want to prostitute myself by doing it for money. For the same reason, later in life, I decided not to play rugby for Wales or become a rock god.

A final memory. In a dustbin behind the security block at the main gate we found a big pile of vicious-looking, heavily-studded belts, obviously confiscated from battling East Camp tearaways. For several weeks afterwards there was a swagger in our steps as we walked around town, studded belts resting on our skinny hips, looking like the Sharks or the Jets in *West Side Story*.

Then we got fed up with having to hide them from our parents and threw them away.

Postscript

One of the great things about Facebook is that it gives you access to all sorts of perspectives that would otherwise be denied to you. I wrote two posts about Butlins (which, above, I've amalgamated into one) based on my own, very narrow, experiences, and was amazed at the flood of other people's memories that they released. Members of the group worked as chalet maids, did bar work, collected and washed coffee-shop crockery, gave advice (from a position of no experience whatsoever) to mothers about the best prams to rent, took on shoplifters as store detectives, shared in the hilarity of guests' holiday snaps in the photography shop, or helped to look after horses and shovelled manure in the camp stables. The memories were invariably positive and life-affirming.

An aspect of the Butlins experience that I perhaps didn't give much, or indeed any, recognition to was its role as a major player in the sex education of the youth of the Llŷn Peninsula. In my defence, naïve mid-teenager that I was, it didn't play any part in my own growing up. But, judging from some of the comments that arose from my Butlins posts, this can't be said of many of my contemporaries. So, although I studiously ignored early nudge, nudge, wink, wink comments, I feel that the time has come to address this issue. Those of a delicate disposition should look away now. Here are some of the comments, for which I accept no personal responsibility:

- Butlins was widely known in the area as 'Billy's Brothel'.

- Some local lads who worked in the camp, after a night in the bars, would head for the female staff annex and simply go along the chalets, knocking at each door in turn. They rarely failed to get what they'd gone for.

- Chalet maids who worked in the East Camp, where all the young male and female visitors were billeted, would report washing lines heavy with used condoms. The equivalent, one supposes, of notches on bedposts.

- There was a weekly shuttle bus, it is reported, from the camp to the VD clinic at the Caernarfonshire and Anglesey Hospital in Bangor.

Given that the camp accommodated thousands and thousands of young single men and women from the big cities of the Midlands and the North-West, intent on enjoying their short summer holiday, together with thousands more families with children, Butlins did a pretty good job of giving each group what they wanted. They segregated them (young men and women in East Camp, families in South Camp), and set up the sort of entertainment that each group might appreciate.

Some further anecdotes from the comments:

- Young man's route from Trefor to Butlins to get to work: bus, car, hearse, van. Don't ask. I didn't.

- Trolley-boy scam: 'Double the tip, and I'll pick your luggage up next Saturday and take it to the station.' Fat chance.

- Bar-customer scam: stand in the crush at the bar, waving

a fiver. When served, substitute a pound note as you hand over the money. Hope to get change for the fiver.

- Local squaddie, with squaddie mates, in camp illegally, rumbled by a security guard and sprinting between chalet lines towards the perimeter and freedom. Cheered on by Scouser, "urry up, lads, e's after yeh!' Scousers always, always, side with the underdog.

- Young lad working with a load of older girls, earwigging their candid conversations about their love life, and learning what to do, and not to do, what to say, and not to say, when dealing with future girlfriends.

- If you worked in the bars, you always ran the risk of getting caught up in the fights that inevitably broke out. Best advice – work out a plan of action for every eventuality and, as a last resort, have an ally behind the bar who'd delay dropping the grill until you could slide underneath to safety.

- The gardeners, I got a distinct impression, were a gentle but quietly subversive section of the Butlins workforce.

  o The story of gardeners, clearing up after a harvest festival event at the camp, smuggling a host of fruit and vegetables out to their widely-distributed homes. The story was specific as to how each vegetable was smuggled. Don't ask about the cucumbers.

  o The story of hundreds of rose bushes being delivered to beautify gardens across the camp, only for a few to disappear as they passed through each level of management, resulting, finally, in four reaching the men who were tasked with actually planting them. The disappeared bushes in turn beautified gardens across the peninsula.

- Finally, a tale of the Pig and Whistle. The staff, it was rumoured, were finding it hard to get drunken customers out after legal closing time had expired. So they paid a man to come into the bar with a huge drum. He'd march up and down, banging his drum, knowing that customers would form in behind him. When the conga consisted of virtually every drunken reveller in the place, like the Pied Piper of Hamelin, he'd lead them in a serpentine dance between the tables and out into the street. When, of course, the staff would slam and lock the doors. This sounds to me like an urban myth, and a recipe for violent staff-customer confrontation. But I offer it for what it's worth.

Newspapers

I haven't read a physical newspaper in years. These days, I read the *Guardian* every morning on my phone, then do a sweep of other news sources, in Britain and from across the world. I must say that I don't have any wish to return to the newspapers of my childhood. They were broadsheets, which, if you had the short arms of a child, were hard to manage without poking the person you were sitting next to in the eye. The content was hardly child-friendly either – articles written in formal English, with lots of big words, about subjects in which you had no interest whatsoever.

The daily paper my father had delivered – the *News Chronicle* – did nothing for me. It was far too serious and full of boring stuff like politics. Likewise *Reynolds News* on Sundays. The bright spot from a kid's point of view was the racy *News of the World*, known for its salacious gossip. Not very appropriate, you might think, for a pillar of the community like my dad. 'The sports coverage is second to none,' he'd explain. Right.

In order to boost sales, newspapers, then as now, would run a variety of extras and add-ons. Some of these were boring – souvenir supplements about the coronation, for example – but others were far more exciting:

- I've mentioned elsewhere Big Chief's *I-Spy*. He lived in a wigwam in Bouverie Street, just off London's Fleet Street, coincidentally the address of the newspaper's premises (and, also coincidentally, a five-minute walk from where I was to attend university over a decade later). If you paid to join the tribe, you got a membership pack which allowed you to decode the messages from tribe members or the big chief himself that appeared in the paper. You could also buy, from newsagents, *I-Spy* booklets about a host of subjects ('On the seashore', 'In the garden', 'Birds'). You earned points, weighted according to rarity, for spotting a variety of things in the booklet, and when you'd completed it and got it signed by an adult, you could send it off and get 'a feather in your cap' and a certificate.

- Another scheme run by the *News Chronicle*, designed to boost sales during the slack summer season, involved a character called Lobby Lud visiting various seaside locations, where members of the public, if holding a copy of the paper, could accost him with, 'You are Lobby Lud and I claim the five pounds.' A lot of money in those days. When it was known that Lobby Lud would be at Butlins Pwllheli, a group of us, who'd sneaked in, bought a copy of the paper then scoured the camp. We hunted as a pack – if we spotted a likely target, we agreed that one of us would grab the paper and do the necessary. We'd then divi up the prize. God, they say, looks at our plans and smiles. Or in our case laughed out loud. All we managed to do was to irritate a string of campers who turned out not to be Lobby Lud.

Newspapers were, in many ways, more appreciated for their afterlife than for delivering the news:

- On a Sunday, I would spread the pages of the newspaper out on the floor and proceed to clean my rugby boots on them: scrape the mud from between and around the studs with a knife, wipe the boots with a damp cloth, then dubbin the leather.

- My father would build a fire by crumpling newspaper up in the grate, top it with concertina-like firelighters made of a rolled-up newspaper, then top those with kindling, coke from yesterday's fire, and finally coal. If the fire wasn't drawing properly, he'd block off the top half of the fireplace with a newspaper, creating a powerful draft of air underneath it. This worked well, though the newspaper occasionally caught fire and caused panic.

- At school we would make puppets by modelling a head out of plasticine, covering it in papier-mâché (made by soaking strips of newspaper in paste), digging the plasticine out when the papier-mâché head was dry, then adding the glove part of the puppet, made out of odd bits of material.

- If you bought crockery on the Maes, the stallholder would wrap it in newspaper for you to take home.

- We would line the bottom of our budgie's cage with newspaper. His name was Chuck.

- Drawers would be lined with newspaper.

- A layer of newspaper would be spread out on the floorboards before laying lino.

- Newspaper would be cut up into squares and hung on a piece of string or a length of wire in our outside loo. In the inside loo, we had proper toilet paper. Posh or what!

- Finally, it is a truth universally acknowledged that fish and chips taste better when wrapped in newspaper.

It's also true that for newspapers to live, great swathes of Scandinavian evergreens had to die. But if you take into account all the other things that newspapers were used for after their principal function was complete, would this not offset the huge environmental cost of traditional newspapers in their heyday?

Almost certainly not.

Postscript

The main themes in the comments on the place of newspapers in our 1950s and '60s lives were:

1. Perhaps unsurprisingly, since we were kids, our main memories of the newspapers our parents read were the cartoon strips: *Fred Basset, Andy Capp, Batman, Rupert Bear, Dan Dare* were all namechecked. My favourite *Andy Capp* cartoon? After a huge argument, Andy says he's leaving his wife Flo, and walks out. Seconds later, he's back. 'How many sugars do I take in my tea?'

2. A whole host of additional uses for old newspapers came up, many of them throwing light on domestic life in Pwllheli at that time:
   - Wrapping things up when moving house.
   - On which to clean and polish shoes.
   - On which to gut fish.
   - Absorbing body fluids under the stairs when the dog was having puppies, or the cat kittens.
   - Wrapping rubbish such as ash from the grate to put in the bin.
   - Packing wet shoes and boots to help dry them out slowly enough not to damage the leather.
   - Covering floors when painting and decorating.
   - Covering tables during art and craft.
   - Keeping oil off the carpet when maintaining bikes or motorcycles indoors.
   - Cleaning windows (often soaked in vinegar).
   - Making a pulp to fill in gaps between floorboards.

3. Others spoke of everyday household life:
   - A child, eventually to join the merchant marine, avidly reading any articles about ships.
   - A young man rising at 6.15 every morning to fetch the papers for his newspaper round from the railway station.

- A dad who bought all the main newspapers first thing on Sunday, then spent all day reading them. His wife's attitude to this was not recorded.

Mentioned several times was the fact that, as kids, we were completely unaware of political bias in newspapers. Over fifty years later, our horror at the rags our parents chose to read is almost comical.

Trips

I'd always thought of a Pwllheli upbringing as being isolated. Yet the more I think back, the more I realise that we didn't do too badly.

- For a start, there were the Sunday school trips. We St Peters Church kids had days out in Rhyl, Colwyn Bay, Llandudno and Barmouth – I'm sure the chapel kids had much the same. We got there by train, a rare treat, giving us the freedom, despite the best efforts of the adults, to roam up and down the corridors and stick our heads out of the windows. We spent the day on the beaches or in the funfairs, and either ate fish and chips from greasy newspaper or felt grown-up ordering meals at café tables.

- Then there were the school trips. From Penlleiniau we went up to Tre'r Ceiri on the Rivals, a stiff climb from the Llanaelhaearn to Llithfaen road up through the sheep-fold to the great Iron Age complex of circular huts and massive walls and fantastic views, and to Black Rock Sands, with a steep climb down the path from the little 'Halt' where we got off the train to the huge sandy beach.

- From YRP the rugby teams travelled to away games all over north Wales, and most years also down to Cardiff Arms Park for internationals. At one Wales v. Ireland match I started to feel faint and rested my head on the back of the bloke standing in front of me. Next thing I knew, I'd been hoisted up in the air and was passed on a rippling sea of hands down to the touchline. I took a dim view of some of those hands rummaging in my pockets for change as I passed overhead, but what a great view I had of the rest of the match!

- Later on, there were the excellent coach trips organised, if I'm not mistaken, by Christine Thornton:
  o We spent a whole long day in Blackpool – I'd date it, by the song ('Telstar') that played constantly over the coach radio, to 1962. My memories of the trip are rather sketchy. While it started sedately enough with mugs of tea on the prom at 5.30 in the morning, it became increasingly chaotic as the afternoon progressed into the evening. I drank cider all day and became very poorly. At the end of the evening, as I threw up outside the pub, a man walking past with his wife said, sympathetically, 'That's it, lad. Get it up!' I nearly cried with gratitude for the warm sympathy in his voice. When I got back to Pwllheli I explained my pasty face and dishevelled appearance to my parents by saying that some oysters I'd eaten had disagreed with me. I'd never eaten oysters in my life. And I've never drunk cider since.
  o A cultural trip to Llangollen was ostensibly to visit the International Eisteddfod, but was, for some of us an excuse to catch a bus to Chirk and have a pint on a Sunday in a pub that straddled the border with England.
  o Finally, and most memorably, there was the trip to see the Beatles in Llandudno – by my reckoning in August 1963 at the Odeon. A visit to a nearby pub, then prime seats in the front two rows with the Fab Four (oh, please, we never called them that) playing their hearts out above us on the stage, almost within

touching distance. Not for us the huge stadium with tiny figures in the far distance that has since become the norm. One of our number overdid it in the pub, became ill, vomited across the floor at the base of the stage, and missed the whole performance. We sang Beatles songs all the way home on the coach.

Liverpool

It was said during my childhood that Liverpool was the capital of north Wales. It was certainly the nearest big city. Although it was a hundred miles away, our townsfolk thought nothing of going to Liverpool for the day – to do Christmas shopping, say, or to go to see a show or a pantomime, attend a football match, or just have a day out.

My own memories include a trip with my father to Liverpool. I remember a ride on the overhead railway (closed in 1956, so I was ten or younger). Designed to get the dockers to their work (its nickname was 'the dockers' umbrella'), the trains on the overhead railway travelled along the Mersey, stopping at each of the docks in turn. To me, a small boy, the rows of great ships were a magical, awe-inspiring sight. (Joke I heard later: Man to docker, 'Where's the urinal?' Docker's reply, 'How many funnels has she got?')

We also, on that trip, made a ferry crossing (to Wallasey, I think, or perhaps New Brighton) – if you didn't get off at the other end, the crossing was free. From other visits *Dick Whittington* and *Cinderella on Ice* stuck in my memory – not particularly fondly, but you've got to give parents credit for trying. On every trip the big stores were an eye-opener – it was in Liverpool that I had my first experience of escalators, pneumatic pipe systems for delivering money and receipts around the store, and self-service cafeterias where you could choose from a wide range of meals on display before your very eyes. I was nearly run over by a bus as I crossed the road diagonally, something I could do reasonably safely in Pwllheli.

Liverpool was the source of the loudest and funniest Butlins staff, who didn't give a toss and were always willing to stand up for themselves. Pwllheli was once thronged with kitchen staff who'd been sacked en masse by Billy Butlin for daring to stand up to management, and an awful lot of those were Scousers. On that day the Whitehall had run out of beer by 1pm. Among campers, groups of Liverpool youths were the most fun and the best tippers.

Many young people from Pwllheli got their first taste of life outside Llŷn in Liverpool. Lads joining the merchant navy went there to be trained and came back with thick Scouse accents. And this wasn't always an affectation – there's something about the Liverpool accent that makes north Walians particularly prone to picking it up. Perhaps it's because it's a mixture of Lancashire, Welsh and Irish. Liverpool was popular as a place for higher education too – my elder brother and his wife lived in Liverpool when they were first married – she studying French at Liverpool University, he teaching in a Catholic comp on Scotland Road. One of my best mates Tony Pierce spent a year at Liverpool College of Art, doing a pre-diploma course, and my daughter studied at John Moores University. My younger brother Chris did his geography degree in Liverpool, too.

Liverpool's allure was unquestionably heightened in the 1960s by the Beatles and the avalanche of groups that they spawned. After all, didn't Ringo Starr cut his drumming teeth at Pwllheli Butlins, in the Rock and Calypso ballroom, where he played with Rory Storm and the Hurricanes? And didn't our local group, who started as the Vikings, became Dino and the Wildfires, and eventually, plugging into the Mersey zeitgeist, record at least a couple of singles as the Wackers?

This might, of course, be regarded as a hopelessly starry-eyed picture of the way Liverpool affected life in Pwllheli. Of course, this big port city threw up its scallies and its violent headcases, as people working security in Butlins could no doubt confirm. I was taken aback when visiting my daughter in Liverpool to see that local off-licences were clad in heavy-duty (bullet-proof?) plastic, and that you had to make your purchases remotely, through a hatch. Yet I also know that, whenever I visit Liverpool today, I feel happy and at home. As I walk along the Albert Dock or visit the spectacular loo in the Philharmonic (not the concert hall, the pub across the road), or view the two great cathedrals over the rooftops, I think: I could live here.

Postscript

The flood of comments after the Liverpool post demonstrated a real affection for the city. I was particularly impressed by one comment which included a quote from Carl Jung – 'Liverpool is the pool of life'. What erudite members the group has, I thought. Then I realised that it came from a plaque in Mathew Street, just down from where the Cavern used to stand, and was probably seen on a visit to a pub called Flanagan's Apple. Other comments provided boozers' notes for a possible Facebook group pub crawl starting at the Crack, though doubts were expressed that a modern-day repeat might, given our age and the likely state of our prostates, prove to be uncomfortable if not impossible. A loo-, rather than pub-crawl. Further comments agreed that Liverpool could be a tough city, but that this in no way reduced its appeal. It even attracted cowboys like Gene Autry and Hopalong Cassidy.

In particular, it was felt that perhaps I hadn't done justice to the Liverpool sense of humour.

- One member of the group reports being on a bus when a Scouser struggled onto the platform carrying a huge side of beef. As he tried to fit it under the stairs, the conductor said, deadpan, 'Most people just bring butties.'
- Another member watched a dolly bird (not PC, but this was the '60s) getting on the bus, made up to the nines. A gallant Scouser gave up his seat. 'Here y'are,' he said kindly, 'Take the weight off yer eyelashes.'

- In the 1980s I visited Liverpool with friends, intending to eat at a well-reckoned restaurant in China Town. Lost, I went into a pub and asked the landlady for directions. She told me how to get there. 'But forget the Chinese,' she concluded, 'Stay here and get pissed.'

- As we walked towards the restaurant, we passed a guy holding a sign directing customers down an alley towards what we'd now call a pop-up shop. 'Lots of bargains,' he was shouting. 'As advertised on Police Five.'

- Much more recently, my wife and I had a city break in Liverpool. We signed up for a tour of the city on an amphibious vehicle – adapted from an American wartime 'duck'. It was a terrific tour, hugely informative, and the pièce de résistance was where it drove down a ramp and out onto the water of the Albert Dock. But the absolute delight of the trip was the quick-fire, laugh-a-minute commentary. Shortly afterwards the same, or similar, vehicle sank, thankfully with no fatalities, and such tours were banned. A real pity – it was brilliant!

Second World War

I was born the year after the end of the Second World War. Yet I don't remember, during my childhood, being aware of this recent worldwide cataclysm. I think I simply assumed that it had passed Pwllheli by. Recent rummaging in the attic of my mind has, however, thrown up a number of echoes of the war that at the time I didn't notice, but which I've since been able to pin down.

Take 'the shelters' at Penlleiniau – passages topped with slabs of concrete that ran between the school and the cliff against which it had been built. They were the main pupil routes for moving between classes – dark clammy tunnels with dank dripping walls. We weren't really aware of their origin – the clue was in the name. They were air-raid shelters.

In school we took, reluctantly, our cod liver oil capsules and calcium tablets, and drank our free milk, not realising that they were government attempts to compensate for wartime dietary deficiencies. I seem to remember, too, horrible concentrated orange juice which was, I think, issued, for the same reason. Then there was rationing. Each week I'd clip the vouchers from my ration book and take them, with my pocket money, to buy my two ounces of sweets in Kampala. Sweet rationing went on till February 1953.

Other memories of my childhood and adolescence were, I now realise, explained by the recent world war: The steel air-raid warden's helmet and gas mask hanging in a cupboard at the top of the house. My parents' loyalty to Williams 80 for groceries ('they were good to us during the war'). The old man reading a Polish newspaper at one of Brexo's outside tables, and the presence of children with Polish names at school. Eventually, too, I noticed the Polish graves in Denio cemetery, and the signs in Welsh, English and Polish in the bars of the Tu Hwnt i'r Afon in Rhydyclafdu, a response to the proximity of the Polish camp at Penrhos.

Physical relics of the war were few. The most obvious was the 'target' out in the bay, put there by the RAF for bomber training. Originally I think clad in wood, it was now a gigantic bare steel tripod. I also seem to remember a concrete machinegun emplacement but have no idea where. And, at the entrance to the harbour next to the wreck of the *Garibaldi*, we scavenged for what we were told were bits of a crashed German bomber.

To another after-effect of the war we were totally oblivious, yet were to have cause to celebrate for the rest of our lives – the setting up of the welfare state. In particular, the Education Act of 1944 and the acts setting up National Insurance, National Assistance and the NHS between 1946 and 1948, were to make us a golden generation, blessed above all others.

The most numerous reminders of the Second World War

were, I now realise, the films we'd watch in the Town Hall and Palladium cinemas – *Sink the Bismarck, Reach for the Sky, Battle of the River Plate, The Colditz Story, The Cockleshell Heroes, I Was Monty's Double* and hundreds more. I remember kids swarming down the steps outside the Palladium, arms outstretched, bellowing out the *Dam Busters* theme, or peering through imaginary periscopes at enemy ships, or throwing imaginary hand grenades, or walking stiff-legged like Douglas Bader.

There seemed to be a law that all British war films had to include Richard Todd, Kenneth More, or above all John Mills. I always had a fondness for John Mills, partly because his older sister Annette was the creator of my hero Muffin the Mule, partly because his daughter Hayley was famous and about my age, but mainly because I'd always thought that he looked like my dad. Once, when I was at university in London, I saw John Mills in the flesh, standing on the steps of the Houses of Parliament. He did indeed look like my father, though (thank you Wikipedia) a little older (two years) and a little taller (one inch).

The main difference, though, I couldn't help noticing, was that John Mills was, compared to my father, far, far better dressed.

Postscript

So many of the comments that followed my earlier posts filled me in on what happened in Pwllheli after I left in the late 1960s. But this post led to lots of images of Pwllheli before I was born:

- A big VE day party, with rides, was held on the Maes.
- Memories of amphibious vehicles ('Ducks') driving along Ala Road, which in turn sparked my own memories of them pulled up on the beach, with soldiers explaining how they worked and kids swarming all over them.
- The proximity of military camps – the Royal Navy's

HMS *Glendower* to the east, RAF Penrhos to the west – together with the fact that hotels all over Pwllheli were requisitioned by the armed forces for the rest and recreation of British soldiers, sailors and airmen, meant that Pwllheli was thronged with servicemen throughout the Second World War.

- These servicemen often fell in love with local girls – two examples given being the fathers of both Tony Pierce and Ian Martin – and passed on stories about their experiences in theatres of war all over the world.

- The last vestiges of the Polish camp at the old RAF base at Penrhos – seems to have been coming to an end with the closing of the Polish home during 2020.

CHAPTER 3:

The Teenage Years

WITH THE COMING of the teenage years, adolescence got into full swing, with all its hormones, difficulties and angst, but also its vibrant excitement and steep learning curve. Our teenage years provided the engine that drove nostalgia for the rest of our lives. This is when we started to dress differently from our parents, to enjoy having our own music, to experiment with the adult delights of smoking and drinking, to take pleasure in the company of the opposite sex. Even, for me, briefly, golf.

In my case, this golden period coincided approximately with the 1960s – from the start of my O-level courses in 1960 to, say, getting married in 1968.

Golf

During the false dawn between lockdowns in 2020, a mate texted me to say that he was about to play his first round of golf in several months. On the same day I saw a video on Facebook of Abersoch golfers back in 1989. God couldn't have made his wishes any clearer. 'Write about golf!'

I played golf on the Pwllheli course from the age of twelve to fifteen – late 1950s, early 1960s. Mum and Dad had taken it up: Dad loved it, Mum not so much. So I got her clubs.

As a junior member of Pwllheli Golf Club I had a locker and access to group golf lessons with the professional, Dick White, at sixpence a session. (Much later, Dick White gave up being a professional golfer to become a teacher, no doubt to the complete bafflement of every golf-addicted teacher on the Llŷn Peninsula.)

I really took to the game. At weekends and during holidays I would cycle up to the golf club and play – usually nine holes, sometimes eighteen – on my own. None of my mates were interested. A summer day, scudding clouds, the smell of cut grass, the sound of the surf and the song of skylarks – it fed the soul. I loved it.

Not that playing golf didn't have its downsides. In a competition in Morfa Nefyn I set off with fifteen golf balls in my bag and had to borrow one from my opponent to finish the round. At that age, I was starting to hit long, but with little control over direction – a fatal shortcoming on the notorious clifftop parts of the course. Anybody who's played Morfa Nefyn will understand.

And back in Pwllheli, on the then tenth hole – a dog-leg around the river – I had the humiliation of having to admit to a sympathetic enquirer standing on the tee above me as I thrashed around in the reeds beside the river, that, no, I hadn't lost my ball, I'd lost my club. It had slipped out of my grasp during a practice swing.

My interest in golf tapered off as I went into the sixth form, side-lined by A-Levels, rugby, underage-drinking, girlfriends and other adolescent pursuits. But though I lost touch with the game, I never lost an appreciation of its beauty. A lad called Parsonage, a superb player, was a contemporary at YRP, and long after I stopped playing I saw him in action at Pwllheli. His perfectly balanced swing, his total control over the ball, were a thing of surpassing poise and elegance. As he disappeared down the fairway, I went into the bar, sat on a stool, and realised that I was never going to be an even passable golfer. I decided to stick to what I was good at.

I ordered a pint.

Postscript

Memories shared about Pwllheli Golf Club were almost universally positive. After all, if you don't like golf, you wouldn't go there.

- My younger brother would, when he was small, caddy for our father. He was no doubt, to quote Wordsworth, 'something between a hindrance and a help'. When he got tired, Dad would allow him to sit astride the trolley for the rest of the round. Back at the clubhouse, they'd play the slot machine, and, when they won, which in my brother's memory was always, he would be taken to John Summers in Station Square, to spend the winnings on Lego.

- A young man turned down the offer of a job as a trainee groundsman at Pwllheli Golf Club. Half a century later he fervently wishes he'd taken it. I'm sure we all have such regrets about some of the roads not taken in our pasts.

- Another young man caddied for 'the big five' – larger-than-life Pwllheli characters. They played 18 holes in the afternoon, a further eighteen in the evening, and swaggered in as the sun set, lords of all they beheld.

- A girl remembers being yelled at for riding her bike across one of the greens. To a golfer, a mortal sin. To a young girl on her way home after a long day at school, and looking forward to her tea, a perfectly valid short-cut.

Smoking

I smoked my first cigarette when I was ten years old, and by the time I got to my early teens I was hooked. Most of my friends smoked too. Looking back, we seemed to spend much of our childhood and adolescence scheming to obtain cigarettes (made harder by their expense) and trying to avoid detection (made easier by the fact that most adults smoked, and therefore had no sense of smell).

My cigarettes of choice were Senior Service when I was flush, Woodbines when money was tight. If particularly strapped, the last resort was Dominoes, which cost sixpence for an open paper packet of four. All were untipped. But I can also remember smoking extra-long filter-tipped Rothmans King Size and Peter Stuyvesant. I associate these expensive cigarettes with long summer days – perhaps holiday jobs allowed me to splash out.

My brother Jeff and I always bought each other twenty Senior Service for our birthdays. In packets of five – if you flashed a packet of twenty, everybody expected you to share. It's to cigarettes I owe the fact that I never developed much of a taste for sweets – all my pocket money went on fags. To that extent, at least, smoking was good for my health.

The big problem arose when the money ran out. You had to rely on filching them from parents' packets left lying around at home. Couldn't overdo it, though – they would have noticed. And, among friends, there was a well-accepted system of quid pro quo where you could borrow fags when strapped and return the favour when flush. But you had to make sure you stuck to the rules – if you got a reputation for borrowing and never lending, you were sunk. When really desperate, you had to rely on collecting 'stumps' and re-rolling the tobacco with Rizla papers. We'd even been known to smoke tealeaves in pipes, but this wasn't to be recommended – they burned very hot and tasted revolting.

The problem of cigarette supply was eased during family visits. When my Auntie Eva came to stay from south Wales, a whole range of cigarettes became available. Her tastes were exotic, developed no doubt during the Roaring Twenties of her youth. Her daily staple was Craven A. They had cork tips, but no filter – designed, I think, to stop the paper sticking to your lips. For special occasions, her go-to cigarettes were Sobranie

Black Russian (very cool, black, with gold tips), Sobranie Cocktail (in a variety of pastel colours) and Passing Cloud (which were oval). When we were younger she'd just turn a blind eye to the odd disappearing cigarette, but when we got to sixteen she'd secretly pass us some when we were desperate. In our later teens supply problems were eased too by Ian Martin who, though a non-smoker himself, would pass around cigs from his dad's shop. I hope this doesn't sully his memory – it *was* over fifty years ago.

Getting a light could also be a problem. I remember when a group of us, with cigarettes but no matches, followed a smoker all the way around the Garn, desperately hoping that when he'd finished he'd drop the stub without stepping on it. Sure enough, when the time came, he flicked it aside and went on his way. Fervently thanking God who, we reasoned, must himself be a smoker, we pounced, passed it around and lit up. Thinking back, perhaps it was the man and not God that we should have thanked – surely he must have been aware that a gaggle of small boys were earnestly shadowing him, and must have had a pretty good idea why.

Postscript

From the response to the post, it was clear that smoking was widely practised and very popular amongst us teenagers. It combined the attraction of doing the forbidden with the glamour of aping Hollywood stars. Who could forget James Dean looking moodily through the smoke of the cigarette hanging off his lower lip, or Paul Henreid lighting two cigarettes and handing one to Bette Davies in *Now, Voyager*? It gave groups of us a common hobby, and, because it was something that most adults did but kids weren't allowed to, it made us feel grown up.

Several anecdotes painted pictures which not only shed light on our smoking culture, but also made me laugh:

- A group of six schoolgirls at the railway station during

lunchtime, sharing a single cigarette, smoking it right down to the last drag by holding it in a hairclip.

- Another group of girls passing the fags around on the top deck of the school bus from Nefyn, desperately trying to get in as many puffs as they could before school.

- A son fetching cigarettes for parents from a machine, and, as a reward, being allowed to keep the change that was tucked into the cellophane of the packet.

- Several boys smoking French cigarettes (Gitanes or Gauloises) in order to look cool, with the added advantage that they were so strong that nobody would try to cadge them. One even admitted to smoking Gitanes in public, but English cigarettes, which he preferred, when he was alone. The suggestion in some comments that the pungent French cigarettes were also useful in disguising the smell of certain illegal substances must date them as being after I left Pwllheli – wacky backy played no part in my childhood.

- A dad who smoked a celebratory cigar at Christmas giving the habit up when his son told him he looked like the back end of a dog having a poo.

- A female student aiming for a sophisticated look, sitting at a bar wearing a long black dress with plunging neckline, smoking a Sobranie Black Russian fitted into a long cigarette-holder, and lighting it with a gold Dunhill lighter. Students had obviously changed since my day. Omar Sharif came into the story too, though I'm not sure how, or whether I believe it.

Reading all these contributions, another smoking memory popped into my head – the great lengths to which we'd go to get rid of incriminating nicotine off our fingers. Cement walls were good, pumice stones were better. I even remember somebody trying to use acid from the chemistry lab. It did not end well.

Drinking

It seems to me that, as far as alcohol was concerned, the period between the ages of fifteen and eighteen was a kind of magical buffer zone between being a child and being grown up.

Under fifteen you were a kid and looked like one. There was no way of getting hold of alcohol, except for the odd surreptitious Christmas swig at home. Over eighteen, drinking was legal, and where's the fun in that? But the three years in between, from fifteen to eighteen, were an absolute golden age.

It started at fifteen with visits to the Penlan Street off-licence to buy British sherry, then a sober walk to, and raucous return from, the side of the harbour or the shelters on the prom. By sixteen or seventeen, since you couldn't drink in Pwllheli – everybody knew how old you were – it was visits to village pubs all over the Llŷn Peninsula. You got there – Nefyn, Abersoch, Llanbedrog, Cricieth – by bus or, as you got older, in friends' cars. You walked home.

And in the pubs alcohol let you release your inhibitions, hone your banter, outline your hopes for the future and feel grown up. You forged friendships that would last a lifetime and, as you walked back to Pwllheli, sang Beatles songs at the top of your voice.

The pubs I remember (and most, fifty years later, still thank God appear to be going) were:

- Nefyn: the Nanhoron Arms, the Sportsman, the Bryncynan.
- Abersoch: the Vaynol, the St Tudwal's.
- Llanbedrog: The Ship, the Glyn-y-Weddw.
- Criccieth: The Prince of Wales, the Brynhir. The Railway (now The Castle) and the George. For some reason we never used the Marine or the Lion.

Since those days, we've become very aware of the dangers of alcohol – we all know people whose lives have been destroyed by the demon drink. But it didn't half help to get you through the agonies of adolescence!

Postscript

Far from being a catalogue of regrets for the way in which we wasted our youth on alcohol, the comments proved to be a joyous celebration of underage drinking:

- The bearer of a heavy 'five o'clock shadow' at the tender age of fifteen became the go-to off-licence buyer for a range of unbearded underage drinkers. He didn't say if he charged a commission for this admirable public service, but he surely deserved to.

- The list of pubs I used to frequent was comprehensively supplemented by others, leading to a sort of young boozers' guide to the Llŷn Peninsula.

- There was also a sadder list of pubs that have since closed, a catastrophe which has, in recent years, gathered pace, and which succeeding generations will find it hard to forgive.

- A particular mention was made of 'The Ring' in Llanfrothen, which was packed out on the Lord's Day with revellers escaping from nearby dry-on-Sundays Dwyfor.

Dating

Reviewing my Facebook posts over the last year, it occurred to me that I've missed out one important aspect of growing up in Pwllheli, the elephant in the room as it were – dating.

The inescapable fact was that what you might call the 'dating pool', in a town of 4,000 perched on a narrow peninsula jutting out into the Irish Sea, was very limited. Realistically, teens were confined to other teens of roughly the same age and approximately the same geographical area. Wide disparities in age were frowned upon, provoking accusations of cradle-snatching. Nobody had cars, and buses were expensive. The usual age gap was two years. One of the teachers at YRP used to read out the names of boys in the Upper Sixth to his fifth form and note the screeches of laughter/embarrassment when the name of boyfriends of any of the girls came up.

'Asking out' could be done in a number of ways:

- Directly, face-to-face. Only for the brave, the insanely self-confident, or the very thick skinned.
- Through friends. Only for those who had friends
- By sending a note. Only for the literate.
- At a dance. Only for those who could dance or were drunk.

Once arranged, a date could take place in a variety of settings:

- The pictures. At the Palladium, double seats were available upstairs, but their cost put them beyond the means of most. At the Town Hall, the cheapest seats were made of wood – not likely to fan the flames of ardour. So most of us would go for seats in the middle price range. For those who were really strapped for cash, the only recourse was to arrange to meet the girl inside.
- Cafés. Usually Brexo, though a good alternative was the one in Abersoch where you were allowed to dance to the jukebox.
- Parents' houses. A rarity which required liberal parents and a fairly big house. Such venues also ran the risk of cross-examination by the adults, or mickey-taking from younger siblings.
- On walks. Around the Garn or around the beach. For the relatively athletic, and best done when fair weather was forecast.
- The beach itself, but only in summer. Frostbite, like hard seats, can be a passion killer.

Dating was all a learning process, a preparation for future grown-up relationships. And when you think about it, what a complicated and fraught business it was, with very high stakes in terms of personal self-confidence, peer-admiration, and general reputation, and with frighteningly high disaster potential.

Pressures on relationships increased during the summer, with nubile young lasses and street-wise young lads flooding in from the North-West and Midlands, coming either on holiday or to work at Butlins. Even the most stable of relationships could founder on this annual influx of temptation. And, something youngsters today just wouldn't believe, there was the crippling fear of pregnancy, best summed up by the old Welsh joke:

1st man: My daughter's getting married.

2nd man: Duw, I didn't know she was pregnant!

1st man: She isn't.

2nd man: There's posh!

Music

For most of us, our favourite music tends to be what was most popular during our teenage years. But those of us whose teenage years coincided with the second half of the 1950s and the whole of the 1960s were surely the most blessed. Subsequent generations might make fun of our clothes, our hair, our moustaches, but they must surely accept that our music has never since been equalled in originality or quality.

The first time I became aware of pop music was hearing Bill Haley's 'Rock Around the Clock' blaring across the town from Studt's fairground (not the best of starts, I'd have to admit). Next, the film *The Girl Can't Help It* on at the Town Hall Cinema, not for the plot or Jayne Mansfield, but for the musicians: Fats Domino, Little Richard, Gene Vincent and Eddie Cochran. This was in 1956, when I was ten.

But then, in the '60s:

- Dances in the Legion Hall, with deafening music

thumping out across the harbour, much louder, for some reason, when the tide was in.

- Dances at the Memorial Hall, Cricieth.
- Alcohol-fuelled fights at both venues.
- The Vikings/Dino and the Wildfires/the Wackers (that's one local group – they changed their name a lot) at both venues.
- Gerry and the Pacemakers and Billy J. Kramer and the Dakotas at the Memorial Hall. Seems unlikely, but I'm sure I remember it.
- A trip to see the Beatles in Llandudno. On a recent family Facebook thread with the next generation ('Most impressive first live gig attended') I won by a mile.
- The Beatles on *The Lenny the Lion Show* (honestly). My older brother pointed at the screen and said, 'That's Ringo Starr, he owes me a cigarette!' Ringo, then drummer with Rory Storm and the Hurricanes, came out of the Rock and Calypso in Butlins, and cadged a cigarette off my brother, who was sweeping the road outside. If you take into account the proportion of total worth that that cigarette represents, I reckon Ringo owes by brother several million quid.

But we didn't just *listen* to music – we also *sang*, though I can't make any claims as to the quality of our efforts.

My main memory is of singing Beatles songs. An illustration. We'd had a night in the Sportsman in Nefyn. We were drinking in the front bar when full-throated singing started spontaneously in the back room. Several tables of domino players, clicking away, had launched into 'Calon Lân', in full harmony, and this was followed by a further selection of favourite Welsh hymns. I don't know if this happened often in the Sportsman, or if it was a one-off, a local choir perhaps enjoying down-time after a rehearsal, but it was beautiful and completely spontaneous. So, inspired by that uplifting experience, we walked home to

Pwllheli (seven miles – what it is to be young) singing every Beatles song we knew, at top volume and in full harmony.

Our favourite Beatles songs were the call-and-respond types, not actually written by Lennon and McCartney ('Boys', 'Money', Twist and Shout'), but we also had a crack at the more nuanced and more difficult Top Ten singles. Because the Beatles didn't write songs to a formula, we often didn't like them when they first came out – each one was completely different from the previous one – but they grew on us. Today, over half a century later, there isn't a single Lennon-McCartney song from that time that doesn't, without fail, conjure up a specific memory of my growing up.

Non-Beatles popular songs were confined largely to the coach taking us to away rugby matches. Some, usually led by the older boys, were hit parade songs by the likes of Elvis Presley and Buddy Holly – slightly before our time. One was a Nina & Frederik song ('Listen to the Ocean') which games teacher Harry Hughes came all the way to the back of the coach to tell us was one of his own favourites. It must have been – he rarely ventured to the back, being aware that everyone was smoking but, like Nelson, choosing to turn a blind eye. One of the many traits we loved him for.

We also sang non-pop songs. For example, 'When the Welsh revolution comes', sung to the tune of John Brown's Body: Two verses I remember: 'We'll make Sir Winston Churchill smoke a woodbine every day,' (fair enough) and 'We'll make Aneurin Bevan wash the steps of Transport House' (shame, shame). The chorus was always, 'Free beer for the schoolboys' (three times) and each verse and chorus ended with 'When the Welsh Revolution comes'.

Other songs reflected Llŷn's main industries. Farming was represented by 'Gafr wen' ('white goat'). Roughly translated, it went: 'Is there a white goat? Yes, and it hasn't been milked. On the sharp rocks the old goat is wandering,' with each round adding a different coloured goat, and with the tempo speeding up progressively until the whole renditions collapsed in hysterical laughter. They don't write them like that any more. Seagoing was represented by 'Fflat Huw Puw', the story of Huw Puw's boat setting sail from Porthdinllaen, whose translation is beyond me ('Huw Puw's boat is sailing tonight, the sound of raising anchor, I want to go to sea' is the best I can manage). I can only imagine we learned it at school.

I always think of north Wales as the land of poetry, and south Wales as the land of song. But, song-wise, we didn't do too badly.

CHAPTER 4

Friends

THE SWIRLING EBB and flow of childhood and adolescence took place against a number of backdrops. Probably the most important of these was friends.

As I grew up in Pwllheli, I knocked around with nine other lads of around my own age. We were loosely known as 'The Boys'. Amongst ourselves, at least. What I remember of each of these mates in no way reflects how close I was to them – the memory, like God, works in a mysterious way. I can understand why Ginge inspires so many reminiscences, of my own and others – he was a larger-than-life character whose time on earth was all too short. Tony and I were the only two of the boys to be in the same year – the rest, though only a few months younger, were in the year below – so it's inevitable that lots of my memories are about the two of us. But we all – myself, Ginge, Tony, Garnett, Brian, Steve, Mop, Dil, Joe and Jonesy – spent so much time in each other's company that my stories and memories of each overlap and intertwine. Two others – David Morgan and Brian Kerr – weren't part of 'the boys' because they were two years older. David was Steve's brother; Brian was a late arrival in Pwllheli. But they both had a big influence on our lives, so deserve to be included here.

Ginge

A recent obituary of Peter Martin, encountered whilst surfing the Net, released a flood of memories, not of Peter, who was my older brother's age and who I didn't really know, but of his younger brother Ian (Ginge). He was one of 'the boys', and his early death – shortly after we'd all left school – in a way defined our youth and marked the end of our adolescence.

Ginge was unique, one of life's eccentrics:

- He used to smuggle out bundles of bangers from his dad's shop in Gaol Street so that we could sit at the top of the huge tidal harbour gates under the Cob bridge, light the firework bundles then drop them fizzing into the water. They'd sink out of sight then, seconds later, explode like depth charges, with a flash of light, a deafening boom, and a great eruption of smoke boiling to the surface. Just like depth charges in the war films about submarines that we loved.

- The first time I ever got drunk was at the age of fifteen with Ginge. We sat on the sloping harbour wall near the Legion and shared a bottle of British sherry from the off-licence in Penlan Street.

- In pubs, during subsequent years, he would enter a pub and, pointing at the ranks of bottles behind the bar, order, 'Some of that yellow stuff,' or, 'Some of that green stuff.' He was no connoisseur.

- Another time he blithely ordered, 'A scotch and whisky,' The barman served him a double Bells, then drew Garnett aside, nodded towards Ginge and said, 'Is he eighteen?'

- In our later underage drinking period, a group of us were sitting at the front lounge window of our favourite pub, The Railway, in Cricieth. It was early on a hot summer's evening. Ginge, sitting on a stool, picked up his pint, took a swallow, then leaned back, expecting the window to be closed. But it wasn't. He slowly and majestically toppled out into the pub's front area. He smiled ruefully and climbed back in, somehow not having spilled a drop.

- Ginge decided to build a bomb to blow up some of the bass (or was it mullet?) that inhabited the shallows in different parts of the harbour. Where he got the knowledge to do this in pre-internet days I've no idea. But he held on too long, and it blew off his middle finger and half of his index finger. When he eventually got back to school from hospital, Llew, our Latin teacher, drily said, in relation to Ginge's role in the school first XV, that he'd now have to hook with his feet.

- Ginge often did a great act of sticking the stump of his index finger up his nose and saying that he was scratching his brain.

- Ginge was a keen amateur photographer who possessed a rare early Polaroid camera. Once, when we got back from a Saturday morning rugby match, he persuaded me to walk through the empty school and join him in the Head's study, where we took pictures of each other sitting in the Head's chair with our feet up on his desk. I have, alas, lost the photos. He also set about photographing teachers in class.

- There was an informal competition going on amongst the lads as to how many stripes of the Head's cane we could accumulate. By the time I left school, my score was nine. Ian's was fifty-six. And he was the year below me, so still had three school terms to go.

- Six of these were for walking down the main corridor on an assembly morning, dragging a huge branch that he'd discovered outside the school, blown down in the previous night's gale. Pupils and staff were having to flatten themselves against the walls to avoid being dragged along. What he had in mind I've no idea, but the Head took a dim view of the disruption caused to the whole school.

- When I was a student in London, Ginge and the rest of the boys came down to visit me in Knightsbridge, sleeping on the floor of my room. As we were coming back from the pub that first evening, Ginge was nonchalantly swinging his ever-present (and very expensive) camera on the end of its strap. It smashed resoundingly into a lamppost. He shrugged and muttered, 'I'll just pick up the big bits.'

- Towards the end of his life, as I understand it, Ian had a minor accident on his motorbike, suffering superficial cuts and bruises. One of the cuts became infected, the infection spread to his kidneys, and he became very ill indeed. He ended up having to attend regular dialysis sessions at a Liverpool hospital. The story he told us was that, whilst there, he climbed down a fire escape (in his pyjamas and dressing gown), and sloped off to the nearest off-licence, returning with a carrier bag full of bottles, which he handed out to his fellow patients. This was in a renal unit. One hopes that none of them suffered any lasting damage.

- At the age of twenty-one Ginge was waiting for a kidney transplant when he died.

Postscript

My two posts about Ginge, combined above, brought forth a deluge of memories in what can only be described as an outpouring of love. This more than half a century after his death!

Some of the comments were embellishments on my own memories. For example, I hadn't realised that his mission to photograph members of staff wasn't simply a matter of taking quick snaps during lessons, but on at least one occasion involved having an accomplice. He primed a girl in his class (one, it has to be said, who was no stranger to strife in her relationship with teachers) to wind up the notoriously highly-strung Bono. This she duly did and Bono went spare. Ginge got his photo. She got sent out.

Other comments added stories I'd not heard – for example, of sawing through the leg of the Head's desk, or of setting fire to a chemistry lab and an art room. None surprised me, though I doubt whether any of them were done maliciously – they were far more likely to have been the result of his hare-brained *Just William* type schemes.

Talking about hare-brained schemes brings me back to the ill-fated fish-busting bomb. I said in my original post that he'd held onto the bomb too long, which implies some sort of timer. This was not, I now discover, the case. Having built the bomb, Ginge had designed an ingenious way of setting it off. It was attached to a battery, with the contacts between bomb and battery held apart by an Alka-Seltzer tablet. When he'd lowered the bomb into the water, he would be able to retreat to a safe distance, the tablet would slowly dissolve and in due course the contacts would meet and the bomb would go off.

What could possibly go wrong?

As he lowered the bomb into the harbour, the tablet slipped out and fell into the water, the contacts snapped together, and the bomb exploded. He was really lucky to have survived.

Is this, perhaps, the only time that Alka-Seltzer ever caused, rather than alleviated, a headache?

(Note: I thought very carefully about this ending to the post. Then, as I was doing so, I'm sure I heard Ginge laughing from beyond the grave.)

Tony

Of all the boys, I was probably closest to Tony. This is because, as I mentioned before, we were in the same year (and, indeed, the same class), whilst the others were in the year below. Here are a few memories, in no particular order:

- During one morning break, Tony and I were mock

fighting with Ifan Gwyn Jones, a bit of fun which included breaking a large clod of earth over Ifan's head. As (bad) luck would have it, this was going on outside the art room. As (even worse) luck would have it, we had art next. With Ifan's dad, Cama. Once in class, the fuming father lost no time in avenging his son. Tony, luckily for me (though not for Tony) was closest, and he bore the brunt of a verbal and physical assault. By the time Cama got to me, the storm had blown itself out, and I suffered no more than a half-hearted reprimand.

- Then there was the maths homework. Neither I nor Tony had done it, and we explained to our teacher Maldwyn that we'd left our maths books at home. The normally fierce Maldwyn accepted this gracefully. This should have aroused our suspicion. Suddenly, when we'd lowered our guards, he pounced on Tony's desk and hauled up the lid. On top of the pile of books inside was the incriminating maths book. Tony was taken to task, again both verbally and physically. Peace returned. Just as I was once again beginning to relax, Maldwyn pounced on my desk. No maths book! I looked elaborately innocent and hoped that he wouldn't go through all the other desks in the room – I'd asked, and been granted, Nan's permission to hide my book in her desk.

- Tony and I were in our form room (in the white huts) at break, kicking a ball around. I swung at it, miscued, and it smashed a light bulb high overhead. I trooped off to own up to the headteacher. When asked how it had happened, I offered the best excuse I could think of at the time – I was passing a book to Tony, and it slipped. Even I realised it was weak. I think my three strokes of the cane weren't so much for smashing the light bulb as for offering an insultingly silly excuse.

- In the Sixth Form, as our time at YRP drew to a close, although our social life still largely revolved around 'the boys' and Expresso and visiting pubs in villages outside Pwllheli, Tony and I, because we were a year ahead of the others and approaching school-leaving age, tended to find common cause. We'd take long walks around the beach or up to Gimblet Rock, even in the foulest weather, talking about literature, philosophy, our dreams for the future, that kind of stuff. Or we'd hang out in his parents' hotel, in Tony's loft room, or in the basement, where we'd shoot at targets with his air rifle. We also painted my bedroom in Llŷn Street – he, as consultant designer, chose the colour-scheme (he did art), he and I did the grunt work, and my parents paid for the paint.

- I couldn't work out why Tony was so much savvier than I was. Looking back, it was probably because he was eleven months older. Also, he came into contact with a lot of people from outside Pwllheli in his parents' hotel. I can admit now, though I would have died rather than do so at the time, that Tony was 'cool'. He wore Wrangler jeans, mine were off a stall on the Maes. He made proper coffee in one of those angular chrome coffee-pots you still see around today, I drank Nescafé. He was fit and did weight training. I could hardly move after playing rugby on a Saturday. I was good at doing exams (boring), he was good at art (cool). I would see his sketch book lying open and would love the drawings – of people's faces, or disjointed hands, or the way cloth would drape when worn. He passed his driving test at seventeen, I had to wait until I was twenty-one. He had access to a car. I didn't. Above all, he introduced me to *On the Road* by Jack Kerouac. This was how I wanted to be – a free spirit, a member of the beat generation, drinking and taking drugs, hitchhiking across America, sleeping in strangers' houses.

I've got more stories about after we left school – not only about Tony but about all the boys – but they'll have to wait.

Postscript

Tony contacted me after I posted the above and reminded me that I hadn't paid for his work on my bedroom.

Garnett

Garnett was good-looking, tall, fair-haired, athletic, with an explosive sense of humour. When he thought something was funny (which was often), the laughter would bubble up irrepressibly and spill over, like milk on a stove.

Two indelible memories:

- When I'd finished at YRP and was waiting to go away to college, Garnett (who, as I've said, was a year behind me) was off school. This would have been in September 1964. So we were both at a loose end. Each day I'd call in at his house in Morfa'r Garreg, we'd have a coffee, do the *Daily Mail* crossword, then go out for the day. One morning when I called, Garnett was throwing his youngest sister Peta up in the air then catching her, to her very noisy delight.

'Don't do that,' their mum said, 'she's just had her breakfast. She'll be sick.'

Garnett took no notice, egged on by his little sister who was screaming with laughter and yelling, 'Again, again.' It ended with Garnett holding Peta high above his head – I can picture it now – with him smiling up at her, she laughing down at him. Then she threw up, copiously, directly into his face.

Their mum took Peta from her brother and sat her at the kitchen table, then handed a towel to Garnett so that he could clean himself up.

She didn't say, 'I told you so' or in any way tell him off. But I swear there was the trace of a smile on her lips and a definite twinkle in her eye.

- Garnett was fly-half to my scrum-half in the YRP school rugby team. He was a natural, I wasn't. But I owed him my place in the Caernarfonshire under-fifteens. At the start of the trials in Bangor we were divided into two teams – the probables and the possibles. Inevitably, Garnett was in the first, I was in the second. As the game progressed, the occasional possible was transferred to the probables and vice versa. Garnett was having a terrific game, handling unerringly, kicking accurately and making great runs. But each time he almost got through the probables' defence, I brought him down. At the time I assumed that, being his friend, I was simply not intimidated by his speed and strength. Now, looking back, I wonder if he didn't just let me tackle him, to impress the selectors. Whatever the reason, it got me into the probables and therefore into the county side. This changed my life. Being able to claim to be a 'Welsh county rugby player' on applications for university and then for teaching jobs, did me no harm at all, never mind that it was only the under-fifteens, and that only a handful of schools in the county played rugby.

Thanks Garnett!

Postscript

- Garnett's then girlfriend (later wife, now alas widow) remembers a trip down to London with Garnett, Ginge and Joe. Sitting in a pub, they started to sing a Welsh song and were asked by the landlord to stop. Their indignation was comical – not because they'd been asked to be quiet, but because half the rest of the clientele were smoking pot – in their eyes a far more serious offence.

- Regarding the story of Garnett throwing his sister up in the air, further thought makes me realise how slippery and unreliable memory can be.
  - o The likelihood of our having done the crossword certainly seems to have been corroborated – his widow

97

> Alwena told me that he did the *Daily Mail* crossword throughout his life, and that, after they'd moved to France, she was left with a pile of old copies of the newspaper when he died.
>
> o Other details, though, seem more questionable. My feeling was that Garnett was off school because he'd broken his arm. If that's true, how could he have been throwing Peta in the air?
>
> o Even more worryingly, my memory is of Peta being a tiny giggling infant. Yet I suddenly realised that she was in my little brother Chris's class at school, making her about the same age – I phoned him to check. Which would have made her five or six years old in September 1964. Surely a bit big to have been thrown into the air, especially by a brother with his arm in a cast?

That said, my core memory is clear, and as I described in the post. So perhaps Garnett only broke his wrist, or had recently had the cast removed, and perhaps Peta was small for her age.

Brian

Though all the boys were funny in their own way, there was no doubt that Brian was the most gifted of us as a comedian. As is the way of such things, though, most of my memories of the things he said and did have simply evaporated, like puddles on a hot summer's day. So I'll have to make do with what remains:

- He informed us that a very short person of our acquaintance was suing the council for building the roads too close to his bum.

- Coming out of the Palladium after seeing Elvis Presley in *Flaming Star*, he staggered down the steps, pulled an imaginary arrow out of his shoulder and announced in a

Presley drawl, 'I have seen the flaming star of death, and I'm goin' into the hills to die.'

- He found himself in Pwllheli police station, suspected of driving (I think it was Garnett's car) whilst under the influence of drink. In those pre-breathalyser days, the sobriety test involved walking along a marked straight line, standing on one leg and picking an object up off the floor. The procedure was explained, a coin was thrown down next to the end of the line, and Brian was told to begin. Not in the least intimidated, he pranced along the line pretending to be a fairy, arms curved above his head, stopped dramatically, raised one leg balletically off the ground, whilst gracefully swooping down to pick up the coin. He held it triumphantly over his head, then bent forward in a theatrical and flamboyant bow. All this was done without once deviating off the line.

It is not recorded if the police onlookers applauded, but they certainly had to let him go.

Postscript
An anecdote I hadn't heard before: Brian was walking down Gaol Street with one foot on the pavement and one foot in the gutter. When asked why he was walking in that eccentric manner, he replied, 'I was born on the side of a hill.'

Steven
Steve had a wicked sense of humour, and a knack for pricking pomposity:

- In the Town Hall cinema the tickets for the front few rows of seats (as already mentioned, wooden, with no upholstery) cost only a shilling, and were usually the exclusive domain of us kids. One night the unheard of happened, and an adult, looking distinctly embarrassed, sidled to the front and sat down at the end of our row.

Noticing his arrival, Steve cheerfully called out to him, 'Welcome to the bobs' (Historical note: a shilling in old money was commonly known as 'a bob'). I can't remember if this salutation, loud enough to have been heard throughout the auditorium, reduced his discomfort, but I doubt it.

- Steve was an excellent mathematician, and after O-Level went on to do pure and applied maths at A-Level. When asked what he was studying, he would reply, 'Hard sums'. Then, at university (Swansea, I think) he continued with his mathematical education, reading 'Very hard sums'. Finally, the last time I met him, he'd just finished his PhD in 'Really, *really* hard sums'.

Mop

Mop was bright but pretended not to be.

- He found it hilarious that I (a clever grammar school boy) struggled to do the reverse maths required when playing darts, subtracting the score from the original 301, when he could do it effortlessly, and instantly.

- I remember him grabbing, in Brexo, a book I'd won as a school prize (*Autobiography of a Supertramp* by W.H. Davies) and reading out, sarcastically, the first words of the Foreword by George Bernard Shaw – 'I hasten to protest at the outset...' I remember the words still. It labelled me as a pretentious intellectual. And he read the words perfectly, despite his pretence of being a dimbo. And I think he was right.

- Mop was a dedicated user of bad language. He was the only person I've ever known who would break a single word in two, then insert a swearword. For example, I remember him talking about a boat everyone in Pwllheli knew. It had, many years before, put into the harbour with a leak, and after fixing it had proved impossible, had been scuppered. He called it the *Gari*******baldi*.

- Mop and I were out drinking in Butlins. On a visit to the toilet, he staggered out of a cubicle shouting, 'Jos, I've just been sick and I've lost my false teeth'. He indicated his mouth, with Dracula fangs and no teeth in between. My shoulders sagging, I pushed past him into the cubicle, rolled up the sleeve on my right arm and started trawling though the vomit in the toilet, trying not to gag. Hearing laughter behind me, I looked around, and there was Mop, doing a little jig of delight and waving his denture triumphantly in the air.

The last few times I met Mop, I felt he was settling down, and yet was missing his years travelling the world in the merchant navy. Towards the end, he worked for Trinity House, servicing buoys, doing stuff that seemed incredibly dangerous. One of his jobs was to jump off the bow of the ship onto the buoy, and attach a hook to allow it to be hauled on board (to replace batteries? I don't know). In a pub on the front at Felixstowe (he was visiting us in East Anglia), seeing the lights of ships leaving the docks and setting off into the North Sea, he had a sad, faraway look in his eye.

I didn't hear of his death until long afterwards – far too late to attend his funeral.

Postscript

In the comments, a story emerged about Mop that I'd not heard before. In Brexo one Saturday night he went from person to person asking for fourpence ('s gin ti rôt?'), saying that he needed this amount to get the bus home to Morfa Garreg. The person who reported this (still aggrieved after sixty years!) said that he eventually trousered five shillings – for most of us a week's pocket money, and enough for at least fifteen bus tickets.

Dil Beans

Dil Beans was academically bright but had no interest in carrying on his education beyond O-Level. He'd always wanted to join the merchant navy, and that's just what he did. I remember one afternoon meeting him in the Mitre, where he was sinking rum and blacks at an incredible rate of knots. He told me that, after he'd docked in Liverpool, he was so keen to get back to Pwllheli that he did the hundred miles in a taxi! I still don't know if he was joking. Last I heard, Dil was quartermaster on the Irish ferries and living in Holyhead.

Joe

Looking back, Joe reminded me of Arnold Schwarzenegger. And, not only was he big and strong, but playing rugby he was totally fearless. I often thanked God that, because we were on the same team, I'd never have to play against him. Towards the end of the summer holidays Joe would work for Eifionydd Farmers on some sort of grain-drying machine. The work was brutal and the hours outrageous, but in a matter of a week or two he'd make more than the rest of us had earned all summer. Difficult to forgive, that, even in a mate. As with Mop, I heard of his death much too late to attend the funeral.

Jonesy

I was never very sure why Dave, in a country of Joneses, had been singled out to be called Jonesy. I've a vague memory that it was because at YRP, a two-form entry school, kids were allocated alphabetically in the first year, and that Dave ended up as the only Jones in 1B whilst all the others were in 1A. But I may be wrong. Although in later life Dave became a noted civil engineer and travelled the world, he did sometimes do daft things. He once came home from college (somewhere on the English south coast? Portsmouth?) looking as if he'd gone fifteen rounds with Mike Tyson. Reluctantly he told us what had happened. On his way home (to digs? hall? shared flat?) after a good night out, he'd come across a line of bollards. The demon drink persuaded him that it would be a good idea to mount the nearest bollard, then dance balletically from one to the other. It started well. He was sure-footed, almost elegant. Then disaster struck. His foot slipped off a bollard, he pitched forward, and his face and the top of the next bollard came into violent contact.

It's hard to look sympathetic, I find, when you're trying not to laugh.

Postscript

Dave's sister put me right on several of the details in my account:

- Regarding the origin of his nickname I was close, but not spot-on. By the time Dave arrived at YRP it was three-form entry. When he started (late, I don't know why) in the November of the first term, both 1A and 1B (where all the other Joneses had been placed) were full, so he fetched up in 1C – the only 'Jones' there. So he became 'Jones C' or 'Jonesy'.
- The college was in Plymouth, not Portsmouth.

My last two entries in this section weren't really part of 'The Boys' as such. But in many of our activities and escapades they were often there or thereabouts.

David Morgan

David Morgan was Steve's older brother – because of their father's job as manager of W.H. Smith's, they were often known collectively as 'the Smiths boys'. In the early years they were inseparable but, being only two years apart, often fell out, sometimes spectacularly. During these skirmishes, I learned by observation an important life lesson – when family members are engaged in warfare, don't interfere.

The first time it happened was in Church Street. When they were going at it hammer and tongs, a well-meaning passerby tried to intervene. 'Leave that little boy alone,' she said to David, 'you ought to be ashamed.' At which Steve turned on her and gave her a mouthful, telling her to mind her own ******* business and not talk to his brother like that.

This was the pattern on numerous subsequent occasions. David was always on a hiding to nothing – not physically, but in terms of public relations. Not only was Steven a lot smaller, but he was very angelic looking, with a mop of curly hair. Our friend Merfyn's mother used to call him, to his considerable embarrassment, her 'little ray of sunshine'. So, although he was often the instigator of the fights, and entered into them with impressive enthusiasm, it was always David who got the blame and attracted the condemnation of passing strangers. Inevitably, the person who tried to intervene was left red-faced and angry, and tutting at Steve's language, while the two brothers walked off with their arms around each other's shoulders, their disagreement forgotten.

There was only one time when Steve got the worst of things, not the result of a fight but of an accident. We were in the garden at the back of Smiths, each of us involved in our own projects and activities. Steven, doing I'm not sure what, walked into a spade that David was energetically swinging, I'm not sure why. Trying to dig up the roots of a pear tree, perhaps, or hunting for buried treasure. The edge of the spade caught Steve a sickening whack, and his features were immediately hidden by a deluge of blood. Yelling in shock, Steve scrambled over the wide green garden gate which had refused to open, blood pouring down his face and soaking into his jumper. He ran down the alley towards the family flat over the shop. I dread to think what it must have been like for his mum, opening the door to her child, covered in gore.

I don't know what the outcome was. Hospital, one assumes, and numerous stitches. I hope David didn't get into trouble – it was not in any way his fault. I don't remember Steven being disfigured by a hideous scar – presumably, if such there was, it would have been hidden by those copious curls. Though whether it revealed itself later in life I have no idea – I would guess not, given his father's fine head of hair.

Many of my memories of David are mixed up with generic memories of all of us together. I don't remember him at all in school – he was a year or even two ahead of me, and as we all know, older secondary pupils have, as a matter of principle, nothing to do with the younger kids.

My most vivid memory of David, though, and one I'm not proud of, was of him on his first visit home after he'd started at university. It was at youth club in the church hall. He'd returned (from Aberystwyth, I think) all grown up and wearing his college scarf, and he was surrounded by adoring girls, listening avidly to his tales of university life.

I hated him then. At a stroke, I, a senior prefect, a prize-winning exam pupil, a member of the first XV, a contributor to the school history magazine and an all-round good egg, was demoted – just another schoolboy, another nobody. Yes, I hated him.

If you're reading this, David, don't worry. I forgive you.

Postscript

David must have forgiven me – he added a comment to the post, thanking me for finally putting the record about him and Steve straight, but doubting whether his brother would see it that way.

Brian Kerr

For no apparent reason – that's the way the mind seems to work – I suddenly thought the other day about Brian Kerr. Some of my contemporaries might remember him. I don't know what became of him. And I realised that I knew very little about him.

These are the facts, to the best of my recollection.

- He joined YRP late, though I can't remember when. He had almost white hair. He had a younger sister whose surname was Cramb. So Mr Cramb, the bearded head of the family, was presumably his stepfather. They arrived from Inveraray in Scotland, though I don't remember Brian having a Scottish accent. They lived at the bottom of Salem Terrace – Number 8 perhaps. I don't know what Mr Cramb did, or anything else, really, about the family.

- Brian formed a skiffle group, with himself and two others. Brian led the group by virtue of being the proud owner of a guitar, which looked splendid but which he couldn't play. So he'd stand at the front with his guitar slung around his neck and his hand resting on the fretboard. I can't remember the rest of the line-up, just that they played the usual washboard and tea-chest bass. The only song in their repertoire I can remember (in fact it might have been the only song in their repertoire) was Lonnie Donegan's 'Putting on the Style'.

- Brian was the instigator of our very own Old Barnes high jump pit. The athletics season was under way, and we wanted to be able to practise. Next to Old Barnes (a derelict fire-damaged farmhouse on the round-the-Garn footpath) we dug out a rectangle of turf and excavated a pit. Then, over several days, we shuttled back and forth on our bikes between West End beach and the Garn with sacks filled with sand on our crossbars – back into town, up Llŷn Street and along the path to the pit. It makes me tired just thinking about it. When the pit was full, we rigged up a rickety high jump bar and set about becoming the next Welsh (or in his case Scottish) athletics world-beaters.

- When Brian's parents were out for the night (I don't know where his little sister was), we'd all congregate at the house on Salem Terrace to talk, watch telly, and smoke. We did this in the front room, and on hot summer evenings its big window would be open to the street, but with the floor-to-ceiling curtains closed. One such evening, without warning, the curtains flew dramatically apart, and there, with a demonic grin on his face, stood Mr Cramb. 'Got you,' he cried triumphantly. He'd caught us smoking, bang to rights.

- I was standing outside Woolworths waiting to cross the road. What little I had left of my pocket money after buying cigarettes I'd spent on a Crunchie bar. I'd peeled back the wrapper, leaving just enough at the bottom to stop my fingers melting the chocolate, and was holding it casually at my side, waiting for a break in the traffic. Suddenly, the bar was gone, leaving me holding the empty wrapper. And off up the High Street, my Crunchie in his mouth, ran Bruce, Brian's golden retriever. I swear that dog was smiling.

I can offer no satisfying conclusions to any of these anecdotes. None of the members of the skiffle group ever, as far as I know, became world-famous rock gods. None of us high-jumpers became athletics superstars. No dire consequences followed from being caught smoking (for me at least – I can't speak for Brian). The only one that had any lasting effect on me was Bruce's theft of my Crunchie. About that I still feel, sixty years later, a profound sense of grievance.

Postscript

Several comments filled in some of the numerous blanks in my knowledge of Brian Kerr:

- A member of the skiffle group which he started came forward to own up that he was part of the original line-up. He played kazoo until it broke, when he was reassigned to the tea-chest base. They practised in Philip Lee's kitchen. The name of the group was not revealed, nor was Mrs Lee's attitude to these arrangements.

- Brian sewed elastic into the legs of his rugby shorts, to make it more difficult for opponents to tackle him. He also had an older brother who became a sheep farmer in Tasmania. I don't think there was necessarily any connection between these two facts.

- Mr Cramb was an engineer brought in to refurbish Llŷn's water network. When the family arrived in Pwllheli they stayed at Tony Pierce's parents' private hotel, after which they moved to the house on Salem Terrace. Mr Cramb put some work in Tony's dad's way. He (Mr Cramb, not Tony's dad) rode a big black motorbike with one of those cool bullet-shaped black and silver sidecars. He was widely known as 'Y dŷn du' (The black man).

- Reflecting that Brian seemed to be a natural leader (the skiffle group, the high-jump pit, even the purchase of a rugby ball on the never-never I mention elsewhere, were all his ideas), I googled him – surely by now he must be a famous captain of industry. He might well be, but I could find no trace online. There are a lot of Kerrs in Scotland.

CHAPTER 5

Family

As I MENTIONED in the last chapter, friends seemed to take centre stage during our teenage years, with everything else being part of the backcloth against which we lived our lives. Now, in old age, I can see that this wasn't actually true. Family, acquaintances, primary and secondary schools, the 'cast of thousands' that made up the population of Pwllheli, the town and its hinterland, even the rest of north Wales, were all an integral part of our upbringing. Of these, families were perhaps the most immediate, the most persistent, influence.

Big brother Jeff

Being my parents' first-born, my big brother Jeff was the one they practised their parenting skills on. By the time I came along, they'd got better at it.

My father was a lovely man but, being both the Head of, and a full-time teacher in, a local primary school, when he got home he'd really had enough of kids. He was often, shall we say, on a short fuse. Jeff was the eldest, and bore the brunt.

Some examples.

- At the breakfast table, wanting the marmalade, Jeff lifted the jar by the lid. Inevitably, jar and lid parted company, there was a loud crash, and the table ended up covered in splintered glass, shards of china and sticky marmalade. Dad's reaction was volcanic.

- Again, after one of Pwllheli's rare snowfalls, my brother and I got up before dawn, our parents still asleep, and went out to play in the snow. He persuaded me that we should wear our slippers not our wellies, to minimise the marking of the pristine white blanket that had, overnight, magically covered Llŷn Street. To me it seemed like a sensible, even poetic, suggestion. When we came back into the house, feet and pyjama-bottoms soaked, teeth chattering, Dad didn't see it in quite the same way.

As every parent knows, things get much worse with adolescence. Jeff's school reports were a disgrace, he never did his homework, he often got in late at night. But as Dad's irritation mounted, Jeff started countermeasures. He was sullen. He disobeyed. He answered back. Our house became a battlefield.

Then a turning point. On our way to visit family in south Wales, Jeff was getting in some driving practice before his test. From the start, Dad was hypercritical, and Jeff was growing increasingly morose and uncommunicative. Eventually, realising that he'd gone too far, Dad announced that we'd stop for a cup of tea. 'Fetch the stove from the boot,' he said to Jeff, trying to re-establish cordial relations. 'Get it yourself,' Jeff snapped. My jaw dropped and I waited for the eruption. There was a long silence. Then Dad got out, walked around to the back of the car, and took the stove out himself. My jaw dropped even further.

Jeff's O-levels were nowhere near what our parents had hoped for – three passes. On the day the results came out, he stayed in his bedroom in order to appear contrite, refusing breakfast on the grounds that he was too upset to eat. But, with me at least, he accepted his disgrace with impressive equanimity. As I passed his room, he grabbed me and pulled me inside. 'Get me some food, I'm starving,' he whispered. So I went downstairs and made him a pile of sandwiches.

When he went on the Caernarfonshire school trip

to Holland and Belgium (he must have been sixteen, I was twelve), he brought me back two presents. One was innocuous, for our parents to see (chocolate, perhaps, or a souvenir), the other was a cigarette lighter in the form of a tiny handgun. I was ecstatic! So much so that, as a gesture, I immediately visited the doorway at the side of the Town Hall (down the alley from the High Street next to the bank) where, to facilitate a quick fag on my way to get fish and chips from the chippy in Penlan Street, I had hidden a cache of matches. I dug the tin out of its hiding place and dropped it ceremoniously into the nearest waste bin. No more grubbing around for matches for me, I thought. I now had a lighter! And how envious all my friends were when I lit their fags in smoker's corner the next day.

Jeff took up snooker and was soon better than Dad. Same with golf. Dad found this hard to take but bit the bullet, if with bad grace. I started to think that we were through the worst. Then Jeff went away to Trinity College, Carmarthen.

For the first year or so everything seemed to be OK. The calm before the storm.

Then, on the morning that Jeff was due to go back to college after the summer break, I woke up to a blood-curdling scream. I scampered down from my attic bedroom to a scene of total chaos. Mum was outside Jeff's room in hysterics with Dad trying to calm her down. In his room, Jeff was in bed, looking embarrassed. I tried to find out what was going on but was, as usual, ignored.

I later pieced together what had happened. Mum had gone into Jeff's room. 'It's time to get up. Don't forget you're off to college – you've got a train to catch,' she'd said cheerily. 'I won't be going back today,' Jeff had mumbled, throwing back the bedclothes. He, and they, were covered in blood. That's when she screamed.

Dad dashed out to fetch the doctor – like most people, we had no phone. I was eventually despatched to Williams 80 to get me out of the way. As I walked up the High Street a group of Jeff's friends sidled up to me looking shifty. 'How's Jeff?' John Prys (or was it Jeff Wyn?) asked. 'On his way to hospital,' I replied. I couldn't tell if they were appalled that he'd been hospitalised or relieved that he was still alive.

I had to wait until he came back from C&A in Bangor, his broken ankle in a cast, the two large holes in his thigh stitched and heavily bandaged, to get the full story. He'd been out drinking with his mates. 'Wouldn't see them again till Christmas' he'd said defensively. At closing time they'd decided to enter the gasworks on the Cob, climb the ladder on the side of the gasometer, and run around on the top. As you do. There was a shout that somebody was coming, and they all rushed to the top of the ladder. Jeff missed it, sailed out into space, and plummeted to earth. 'If I hadn't been pissed,' he said to me, 'and therefore totally relaxed, I might have been killed.' 'If you hadn't been pissed,' I thought, 'you wouldn't have been on the gasometer in the first place.' But I kept this to myself.

The funny thing is that I didn't hear the full explanation for the gasworks escapade until forty years later, at Jeff's funeral. I'd mentioned the story, severely edited, in my contribution to the eulogies. In the bar afterwards, John Prys finally dotted the 'i's and crossed the 't's. 'We'd discovered that, if you got onto the top of the gasometer, stood right in the middle and jumped up and down, it flexed, like a trampoline!'

When Jeff married Ambo from Cricieth they honeymooned in London. The highlight (oh stop it!) was an evening at the Talk of the Town, the huge nightclub off Leicester Square. Jeff wore evening dress (I've no idea where he got it from), saying, he told me later, that he looked and felt like James Bond. And I could imagine it – he was a good-looking lad. 'The effect was ruined,' he went on to say, 'by the fact that, every time I threaded my way through the tables on the way to the toilets, people flagged me down to order drinks!'

The final anecdote will have to be in outline only – I

Pwllheli: the Simon family in the garden at Llys Pedr. L–R, back row: Grandma Simon, Uncle Owen, Mum; middle row: me, Auntie Eva, Grandma Hughes, Myron from next-door-but-one; front row: brother Jeff.

Abererch Beach: Dad and Bono (YRP Welsh teacher).

Pwllheli Rec: Dad (middle) and TH (YRP science teacher) (right). TH smoking a pipe *and* holding a cigarette!

Penlleiniau: Dad with, in front of him, Yvonne Shaw and, to her left, Mrs Gardiner. Dad had just, apparently, told a joke – hence the hilarity. (© Paul Shaw)

Mum when young.

Auntie Annie May when young.

Auntie Eva when young.

'Macbeth's three witches.' L–R, Mum, Auntie Annie May, Auntie Eva.

Jeff (left) and me on the Garn. My favourite of Dad's pictures of us.

Bloomsbury, London: me in first year at university. The Post Office Tower had just been built, but hadn't yet opened.

Jeff and younger brother Chris in a photo booth. The challenge was, Chris tells me, not to laugh. Jeff won.

Tre'r Ceiri: cigarette break whilst gathering bilberries.

Brexo: L–R, Jonesy, Dil, me.

The Railway in Cricieth (or perhaps the Crown in Pwllheli): Garnett (left) and me (right). (© Alwena Morris)

On the steps of the St Peter's Church Hall: Brian (sherry bottle and cork), me (striped socks), Jonesy (glasses) and Steve (quiff). Top left: Graham, Brian's kid brother.

Will Martin, D W Jones, Gwyndaf Jones, John Humphries, Eric Baum, Graham Wood, Gwyn Jones, Keith Lewis, Len Humphries
Ian Martin, W O Jones, Arfon Jones, Richard Jenkins, Emlyn Thomas, Richard Jones, Garnet Morris, David Thomas Jones

YRP 1st XV 1964–5: Wil Martin (Ginge's kid brother), D.W. Jones (Jonesy), Ian Martin (Ginge), Arfon Jones (Joe) and Garnett Morris. I'd already left for university.

Paris: Tony's Land Rover outside his flat, with (front) my son Daniel, Tony (back), waving. Top right-hand corner, the Arc de Triomphe.

St Peter's Church: son Daniel's christening, with the Revd Huw Pierce-Jones presiding. L–R, Mum, Jeff, his daughter Ceri, my wife Doulla, Daniel, the vicar, me.

Glan-y-Môr café, South Beach. Daniel.

South Beach: daughter Catherine showing off her gymnastic moves.

West End: Daniel and Catherine jumping off the prom wall.

Steps of Penlleiniau school house. L–R, Daniel, Chris, Catherine.

Cricieth Beach: L–R, Black Rock, Catherine, Daniel.

Cricieth Beach: L–R, the castle, Daniel, Catherine.

Cricieth Castle: Daniel, Catherine, with balsa-wood gliders.

Llanbedrog Beach: Catherine and her son, my grandson, Lazaros.

Llanbedrog Beach: Doulla, Lazaros, me.

Llanbedrog: Lazaros entertaining diners at the Glyn-y-Weddw.

Caernarfon Castle: grandchildren (L–R, Niko, Lazaros), enjoying a day's jousting.

Porthmadog: waiting for the train.

Cricieth: youngest grandchild Arianwen.

Back room at Penlleiniau: Mum adoring, and being adored by, two of her great-grandchildren.

Brasso, one of my favourite teachers. (© Catrin Jones)

Doncaster. L–R, me, Buddug and her son Emyr Wyn Jones. The Welsh secret society extends deep into South Yorkshire.

Pwllheli: the house in Llŷn Street where I was born.

Pwllheli: St Peter's Church, nave and chancel.

Pwllheli: Pont Llechi.

Pwllheli: Gimblet Rock.

Pwllheli: town and Garn from the marina.

Cricieth twenty years ago: the extra 'c' blocked out by language activists.

Cricieth: the Memorial Hall.

Cricieth: castle at dusk.

Cricieth: afternoon dog-walkers on the beach.

Tre'r Ceiri: the path through the sheep fold.

The Rivals, spread across the road to Pwllheli like Batman.

Trefor: the quarry.

Trefor: the quay.

Trefor: y traeth.

Nant Gwrtheyrn: National Welsh Language and Heritage Centre.

Nant Gwrtheyrn: view from Caffi Meinir.

Llŷn:
countryside
view 1.

Llŷn:
countryside
view 2.

Abersoch:
windsurfers
against the
background
of St Tudwal's
Island.

Poster for show at the Memorial Hall, Cricieth. (© Pwllheli Grammar School Ysgol Glan-y-Môr)

Unused ticket for Tonga vs North Wales. Dad died that morning, so never got to the match. (© Chris Simon)

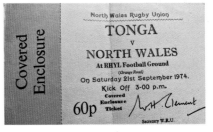

Plaque to commemorate Dad in St Peter's Church, next to the organ.

Dad's pottery, surviving after fifty years and six house moves.

couldn't possibly go into the sordid detail. Suffice to say that, after a night out in Carmarthen at the end of his final college year, which among other things involved an evening of heavy drinking and an altercation with a bouncer, Jeff ended up in the cells and eventually in the magistrates' court. 'I was so embarrassed' he said to me (and it took a lot to embarrass Jeff). The policeman who arrested him was giving evidence. He said that he'd approached 'the defendant', who was 'standing in the middle of the road, singing and waving his arms', told him that he was drunk and went to arrest him. To which the defendant had replied... And at this point the policeman took out a slip of paper and passed it to the clerk to the court who passed it up to the first magistrate on the bench. The magistrate read it, looked shocked, and passed it to the next magistrate. And so on along all five magistrates. 'And the awful thing was,' Jeff went on, 'that Mum and Dad and the principal of Coleg y Drindod were sitting in the public gallery.'

He ended up having to pay a fine and damages to the bouncer. Funny now, but at the time not so much – he was 'rusticated', missed his final exams and had to repeat a year.

Jeff and Dad

During our childhood Jeff always seemed to be in trouble. This experience clearly affected him – for the rest of his life he always had sympathy for the underdog. He worked throughout his career in special schools. He wrote some lovely songs to entertain the kids. And although he could talk about the technicalities of teaching English or maths or whatever to low-achieving kids, his main interest was in preparing them for ordinary adult life, making sure that they could do the things everybody else takes for granted – read a timetable, catch a bus, attend an interview, hold down a job – so that they could live successful, independent lives.

To circle back to our childhood and Jeff's relationship with our father. After Dad died, Jeff and I spent a week helping

Mum to sort stuff out, and most of the time we talked about Dad. We realised that we'd spent much of our early adulthood slagging him off. He was short-tempered. He was a domestic dictator. He was unreasonable. And so on. And on. And now he was gone.

Yet to our wives he was charming and they loved him. To our children he was patient and indulgent and they loved him. To people in Pwllheli he was an estimable man, and they respected him (though some of the Penlleiniau kids were a bit afraid of him). And looking back we realised that, though he could explode at the drop of a marmalade jar, he took his son and heir falling off a gasometer in his stride. In the big things he had a sense of proportion.

By the time he died we were just getting to know him as a person. I'd started going for drinks with him at the Tu Hwnt i'r Afon in Rhydyclafdu, and even, through the 'deacon's entrance', at the Castle in town. As a twenty-eight year old recently appointed head of a small history department in a comp, I'd marvelled at how, four years younger, he'd dealt with the responsibilities of being the headmaster of one of only two primary schools in Pwllheli. Jeff, thirty-two and deputy head of a special school, had felt the same way. It took us being teachers to understand the pressures he faced as a teacher, and us being parents to understand the pressures he faced as a father. It's a part of growing up, no doubt, to start to see your parents as people. Most of us, I guess, go through it.

We concluded that our wives, our children and the people of Pwllheli had been right, and that we had been wrong.

Too late to tell him that, though.

Little brother Chris

Having posted at length about my older brother Jeff, it occurred to me that I really should afford my younger brother Chris the same courtesy. In some ways this is more difficult – Jeff, four years older, was really only a shade ahead of me: Elvis and Buddy Holly, though of his generation, were also part of my early world. Whereas, twelve years younger, Chris's Noddy Holder, though cheerful enough, didn't quite seem to me the stuff of which rock legends are made.

Anyway.

When Mum, at forty-two, got pregnant with Chris, I found the way adults treated her pregnancy, and me, slightly uncomfortable. I was twelve. I can't even remember if I realised what was going on. I just knew that Mum, being well under five feet tall, increasingly resembled a bowling ball. It was excruciatingly embarrassing. But then anything your parents did, at that age, was excruciatingly embarrassing.

My next memory was Mum coming back from Bangor with a baby. I took a mild interest in it, as I would have a budgie or a kitten. Not a puppy – a puppy would have been more fun.

Some time later, Mum took the baby off to Ferndale, presumably to be admired by our family in the South. Chris was pleasant enough before they left, and reasonably easy to look after – you could plant him somewhere and he'd stay there, not yet having learned to crawl, and he took a really intelligent interest in his surroundings. Wherever he found himself, he could keep himself amused.

When they came back six weeks later, it was a horse of an entirely different colour. He could crawl, and not in a sluggish, lackadaisical way, but at a hundred miles an hour. In the confines of Llys Pedr's narrow corridors and diminutive rooms this was terrifying. I kept trying to corral him, but he charged around like a cupid on Speed, his golden curls bouncing. Soon, I was sure, he would collide with the sharp edge of a piece of furniture and die in a torrent of his own blood. AND I WOULD BE BLAMED!

As he got older, Chris became what I can only describe as a cutie. He was extremely pretty, with a phenomenal command of the English language, and an oddly old-fashioned air. At six he could identify and name virtually every car on the road. I stumped him only once. I pointed at a Triumph Mayflower, a curiously angular car that looked like Kryten in *Red Dwarf*. He thought hard, and eventually came up, tentatively, with, 'A Triumph Daisy?' Not a bad try. His other slight mishearing of things are part of our family's lexicon to this day: 'I want a piece of quiet!' and, 'It's the blom on the back!' (It was a 'blond' on the pillion of his tin scooter.)

By the time I was sixteen I was keen to take my little brother with me to Brexo every Saturday morning. Not because I wanted to earn parental brownie points, or because I was a particularly good brother, but because this very pretty, insanely articulate moptop was a cast-iron babe magnet. Instead of being ignored, I was immediately surrounded by girls billing and cooing and chucking him under the chin. Not a puppy, to be sure, but not at all a bad substitute.

I was a terrible brother. I teased him mercilessly. I provoked him into paroxysms of fury to record it on a hidden tape-recorder. I berated him on Tre'r Ceiri when he denied having eaten any of the bilberries we were collecting, despite his virulently purple mouth.

But he was a huge favourite with my girlfriend-then-wife, and became, and still is a half-century later, a huge favourite with my children and grandchildren.

An anecdote to finish. After I'd visited Pwllheli with my family, I got a phone call from my children's school. The Head was perturbed – my kids had told her that, whilst we'd been in Wales, their Uncle Chris had taken them to an ancient site and made them join the National Front! I was able to reassure her.

He'd taken them to Penrhyn Castle, and they'd joined the National Trust.

Three sisters

Pwllheli was a great place in which to grow up. But, thinking about my mother and her two sisters who fetched up in the town towards the end of their lives, I wondered if it was an equally great place in which to grow old.

Mum had been born and raised in Ferndale, a pit village in the Rhondda. On her marriage in 1939, she moved to Pwllheli, where her new husband (my father) had been headteacher of Penlleiniau School for the previous five years. By various routes two of her siblings – Auntie Eva and Auntie Annie May – joined her, and the three sisters ended up seeing out their time on earth together in Pwllheli. I can't now ask them how they rated the town as a retirement destination (they're long gone), so all I can do is look back and draw my own conclusions.

So, by the late 1970s, the three sisters lived, separately, in Pwllheli. Two were widows, one had never been married. They were almost guaranteed a long spell in God's waiting room – my mother's family are very long-lived. I pray that I've inherited my mother's genes, and not my father's.

Mum owned the Penlleiniau school house on Salem Terrace. Auntie Eva, a retired primary school teacher, bought a ground floor flat in Talcymerau Mawr. Auntie Annie May, who'd run her own hairdresser's business in the Rhondda, bought an end terrace in Church Street.

'Macbeth's Three Witches', as Mum once called them, didn't live in each other's pockets, but must surely have been a source of comfort to one another. They could 'drop in' on each other for a chat, meet for coffee in Nana's in Market Square, or the Long Room in Gaol Street, mull over their lives, catch up with family news. Mum and Auntie Eva would do the *Daily* and *Sunday Express* crosswords and consult by phone over any tricky clues. Auntie Annie May and Mum were both on the rota for flower arranging at St Peter's Church. When their brother William Owen was visiting with his family from south Wales, the three sisters would gather at Mum's house (because it was the biggest). When I was home, I would often take all three out to lunch at the Cliffs in Morfa Nefyn, or the Glyn-y-Weddw in Llanbedrog.

The dynamic of their relationship was interesting. Mum looked up to Auntie Eva; Auntie Annie May irritated her. Over the twenty years or more that they grew old together, they settled into a sometimes querulous but, I like to think, satisfying old age. Mum revelled in owning her own house for the first time in her life (the church had allowed Dad to buy it a year before he died) and being independent. Auntie Eva, vivacious, active and still batting away male admirers, read her books and eked out her twelve cigarettes a day. Auntie Annie May loved her tiny cottage and walked her dog around the beach and around the Garn. Looking at sepia photos of them when they were young, I could see that all three were good looking, and never lacked for suitors. Auntie Eva, who'd sent one fiancé packing because he failed, when my grandmother had been very ill, to ask after her health, and broke our hearts by turning down another who owned a brewery, was a huge favourite with us kids, treating us as adults even when we were very little. I was rude to her when I was six, and I still, nearly seventy years later, curl up with shame at the memory. Auntie Annie May was deeply eccentric, used to wear culottes and a leather pilot's helmet, and once owned a pet monkey (called, my brother Chris informs me, Koco). Chris sent me a colourised photograph of her when she was young – what a cracker she was!

They all loved living in Pwllheli – the beauty of the Llŷn Peninsula must have been a welcome contrast to the bald hills, grime and heavy industry of Ferndale and the rest of the Rhondda's pit villages. They got lots of visits from relatives from the South, and never tired of showing off the area – Pwllheli, of course, but also Llanbedrog beach, Nefyn, Whistling Sands, Cricieth, Portmeirion.

Each time I went home, I'd dutifully take my kids around to see them, so that they could be mugged for pocket money. Auntie Eva became increasingly reclusive and grouchy. Auntie Annie May lost her battle with Alzheimer's and didn't know us the last time we visited. Mum stayed remarkably compos mentis, living in her own house (with support), and retaining, by and large, her sense of humour. She even accepted with grace the hallucinations resulting from her macular degeneration. Towards the end, she stopped going to church – oddly, the closer she got to meeting her maker, the less time she seemed to have for him.

So, on any review of good places to which to retire, how does Pwllheli fare? Pretty well, I'd say. The three sisters enjoyed the huge variety of walks, the cafés at which to meet, the security of living in a close community, the frequent visits from, and sense of being envied by, other members of the extended family from the South. Above all, however much they sometimes grumbled, their common memories of a happy childhood bound them together. Yes, towards the end, they felt that the world was going to hell in a handcart, but then don't we all?

Only downside? The nearest general hospital was thirty miles away.

Auntie Iris

Auntie Iris was my father's sister. She played little part in our childhood, yet the few memories I have of her make me like her and bring a smile to my face. Even her funeral. More of that later.

- Auntie Iris never forgot our birthdays and Christmases. And her presents were always memorable, if sometimes a little hit and miss:
  - o Hit: a box of chocolates for me. Imagine – an adult who noticed that my favourite Milk Tray sweets were coffee creams, and had bothered to seek out a whole box of them.
  - o Miss: a *Roy Rogers* annual, not long before I got married.
  - o Hit: two cartoon (*Tom and Jerry*) radios for my young

son and daughter. They loved them. Probably worth a fortune now.

o Miss: a plastic ship in a bottle, my wedding present.

• On her rare (only?) visit to Pwllheli, my brother Chris was sent to meet her off the bus in the Maes. With a pneumatic sigh the bus door opened, and Auntie Iris spilled out, falling down the steps, helpless with laughter.

• Auntie Iris's three children were all different, a sign, surely, that good parenting has allowed them to grow in their own way, to march to their own drum:

o Merlin, the eldest, I don't remember at all, but what a magic name! He emigrated to Australia on a £10 assisted passage, hated it and saved the money to get home. When he got home, however, he realised that he hated Britain even more, and re-emigrated.

o Clarice, who I knew better because she came to stay with us for a while, and whom I liked a lot. During my preparations for my exams (O-levels, I think), I persuaded Dad that it was his duty to his niece to let me off revision and take her to a dance at the Legion Hall. Abandoned by me as I sought out my friends, she took it in good part, saying, 'Now I realise why you wanted to come out.' She eventually married a lad who became the *News of the World*'s regional darts champion for south Wales, a wonderful achievement but not without its dangers – he told me that during away matches he had to be accompanied to the toilet by two heavies from his own supporters, to stop opposing heavies breaking his fingers.

o Auntie Iris's youngest – William – I had never met until his mother's funeral. And that brings me to one of the most extraordinary days of my life.

Auntie Iris had died in Bridgend, and my brother Jeff and I attended the funeral. We hooked up at Auntie Iris's house, where we met William for the first time. He proudly showed us his motorbike – a gigantic Kawasaki 1300. 'I heard that you're a biker,' he said to me. 'Take it for a spin!' I turned down the offer on the grounds that riding my little 50cc Honda on a provisional licence hardly qualified me to wrestle with his beast of a machine, and also that I didn't want to die. So instead he took Jeff for a spin. When they got back, my brother stiffly got off the pillion, and complaining that he had cramp in both buttocks.

After the funeral service, we all went to a nearby pub. William's friends – all bikers – joined us, one of them on crutches, another with his arm in a sling. 'This is absolutely typical,' Clarice told us. 'They have a ward set aside at the local hospital, just for them.'

William then chipped in a story about one of their number. Out riding in the country, he'd come off his bike, but didn't want to be questioned by police – he'd had a fair bit to drink. So he hid his damaged bike behind a wall, which he then hopped up onto to await the appearance of the constabulary. When they arrived, they immediately asked after the whereabouts of his motorcycle. Astonished, he asked them how they knew that he had one. 'You're still wearing your helmet and gauntlets,' they explained, trying not to laugh.

The afternoon of the funeral developed into quite a session. Jeff and I, both living in areas where pubs closed for the afternoon at half past two, upped our consumption as the dreaded bell approached. No shout of 'Last orders'. No bell. Same thing happened at three, then half-three. By the time last orders were finally called – at ten to four – we were feeling no pain. Which was also true of the rest of the mourners, and they didn't have ignorance of Bridgend's licensing hours as an excuse.

Back at Auntie Iris's house, after a buffet, everyone had a nap. There were bodies on every flat surface in the house, and on floors and stuffed into corners. As the afternoon wore on, people started to drift away. Finally, mid-evening, those of us who were left were loaded into a minibus and taken to a pub on the coast, where the wake continued. On the way back to the house through Bridgend, we pulled up at traffic lights next to a pub. The garden at the front was lit up like a stage set, and in it the most terrific fight was under way. Fists were flying, bottles and glasses were being hurled, chairs were being broken over heads. Then the lights changed and the whole tableau slid behind us, to be swallowed up by the dark.

As I returned home on the train the next day, trying to keep my breakfast down, I reviewed my (patchy) memory of Auntie Iris's funeral. I'd reconnected with Dad's branch of the family, and I really liked them. What little of Bridgend I'd seen, I also liked. Above all, I felt that we'd seen Auntie Iris off appropriately in a way of which she surely would have approved.

Perhaps, in the end, that's the best any of us can hope for.

Postscript

- My brother Chris filled in more details of Auntie Iris's explosive appearance on the Maes. Her fall down the steps of the bus was, to her credit, the result of good manners – she was turning to thank the driver when she lost her footing and fell. She ended up in paroxysms of laughter, stuck in the bus exit with her legs in the air, her body jamming the pneumatic doors. Trying to paint a picture for me, Chris likened her to grandma in a *Giles* cartoon. As the driver tried to extricate her, the rest of the passengers had to leave the bus through the emergency exit at the rear.

- My friend Tony Pierce's comment about Auntie Iris's funeral is worth quoting in full:

'An inebriating trip through a world of British quirkiness and the tougher venues of south Wales iron and coal towns. All that is missing is Marlon Brando or Brendan Behan.'

Should 'Auntie Iris's funeral' ever be made into a Hollywood blockbuster, I'd be delighted with this as a review:

The son of a preacher man

OK, I wasn't the son of a preacher man. But it kind of felt as if I was. As part of my father's job as Head of Penlleiniau, he also had to play the organ and run the choir in church. He was even the vicar's warden, whatever that meant. Not a preacher, then, but his high-level church profile did affect my life.

For a start, I had to go to St Peter's three times every Sunday – morning (English), afternoon (Sunday school) and evening (Welsh). I've hated Sundays ever since.

There were other effects too. Several of these concerned the church organ which Dad played, every Sunday and during baptisms, weddings and funerals.

The organ at St Peter's had two keyboards, one above the other and a range of stops on either side, together with a large wooden keyboard on the floor, which he played with his feet. When he sat down at the beginning of the service, he'd switch the fan on and set the stops. I know this because, when I was tiny, I would sometimes occupy the bench next to him. I don't know why – perhaps it was on days when Mum couldn't take me to church and I was too young to go on my own. I have a vague memory of turning the pages of the sheet music, with Dad nodding when the end of each page was approaching. I'd guess that this was a way of keeping me occupied. With certain stops out, he'd play on one keyboard and the other keyboard would shadow what he was playing, as if the invisible man was sitting next to him, joining in. There was a mirror above the console which allowed Dad to keep track of the progress of the service.

Occasionally a man would arrive at church to tune the organ. In order to do this he needed somebody at the console. This was my job. Since I neither played nor read music, he'd write the names of the notes on the keys in pencil, then disappear to clamber about among the pipes that filled the south transept. He'd call out a note (and sometimes a stop, which was difficult – their names were in Gothic script). I'd play the note or pull out the stop, and he'd tap away in the depths of the organ, the note changing slightly until he'd got it right. Dad paid me half-a-crown for two and a half hour's work, which was pretty good pay at the time, especially for a kid.

Sometimes, after the evening service, Dad would forget his glasses. On these occasions, he'd send me to fetch them – we lived a five-minute walk away from the church. Creeping through its dark, echoing emptiness was not my idea of fun – I'd approach the organ, grab the specs, then run like hell.

Although at the time the influence of the church seemed to me to be entirely negative, there were in fact several positives:

- Sunday school trips took us annually to places like Barmouth, Colwyn Bay, Llandudno and Rhyl for the day.

- The Youth Club ('Cymru'r Groes'), was held in the church hall, run by the curate, Mr Willcox. Without it, I would never have learned the Gay Gordons (not a lot of use during Legion Hall and Memorial Hall dances, when all you wanted to do was jive), nor the curious pattern of steps that the Shadows did when they were playing. It was a good place, too, to practise our banter with the opposite sex. Or so I like to think.

- Towards the end of my time as a choirboy, we even got paid. Half-a-crown per appearance.

- There was, too, an annual summer fair. For one, Dad ordered a huge metal tank of goldfish, which he emptied into our bath whilst he divided them up into bowls. They were prizes for one of the stalls – not allowed now.

I never felt that Dad's insistence on our three-times-a-Sunday attendance at church was driven by piety or a belief in God. I think it was just that, given his position, it would have looked bad if his kids didn't go. My enforced attendance came to an abrupt end when I was working for my A-Levels. I explained that I really needed Sundays for revision, and he immediately granted me an indefinite exemption. No flies on me – I realised that, in Dad's eyes, education would always trump the life to come.

What did the grown-ups do for fun?

And no, I don't mean that. Though it clearly went on, otherwise we wouldn't be here.

No, I'm talking about hobbies and pastimes. In a small town like Pwllheli, what could adults possibly do to pass the time? I can only go by my childhood observations of my parents:

- They went to the 'pictures'. Twice a week, without fail. Though not together. In both cinemas (the Town Hall and the Palladium), films were changed on Mondays and Thursdays, so that's when they attended – a choice of two films twice a week. And in both cinemas there were two 'houses', the first starting around 5pm, the second at 7.30. Dad would go to first house, on his own, Mum would go to second house, with a friend (Mrs Hughes from Whitehall Cottage down the road). I assume this arrangement was to save having to organise babysitters. Or just to get away from each other.

- They listened to the radio (a large contraption with glowing valves that had to be switched on five minutes early to 'warm up'), and eventually, when we finally got a set, watched TV. This was done in the dark, the programmes chosen from the weekly *Radio Times* dressed in an embroidered cover.

- Every Friday night they played cards with Mr and Mrs Hughes (yes, from Whitehall Cottage). Every time the door of the room opened thick clouds of cigarette smoke would billow out into the rest of the house. They played three games – canasta, casino and crib – very typical of their generation. That they all began with the letter 'c' is probably a coincidence.

- They both read a lot, exclusively crime fiction, fetched from the town library. When I entered my teens it was my job to change the books. Thinking I might contribute to their self-improvement, I would slip in the odd non-fiction book or mainstream novel. They took a dim view of these well-meaning efforts though, telling me sharply to stick to Agatha Christie, Ngaio Marsh and the like. Anything with a dagger on the spine was OK.

- As with most women in those days, Mum had little time for anything beyond looking after the family. And as with most men, Dad saw time outside his job as his own, to do with as he pleased. Although denied the traditional male pastime (the pub) because he was head of a church school, he still managed to fit in a fair few hobbies:

  o Mum told me that (before my time) he made handbags. This was intended to be a nice little earner, but it never worked out – he couldn't bring himself to accept money, so gave all the bags he made away.

  o For a while he got into fishing. Bought the equipment – rods, reels, floats, weights, hooks, creel and so on – and loved the peace of sitting on a riverbank, contemplating nature. He liked the *idea* of fishing. Then he caught a fish – a small brown trout. Faced with having to kill this beautiful sleek little creature, he chickened out, and never went fishing again.

  o Photography was a much longer-lasting enthusiasm. He set up a darkroom in the cellar, built his own enlarger using an old camera and spent a lot of time taking pictures. To this we owe a collection of rather good photos of us as kids (which Mum loved) and of bent nails in fenceposts (which she didn't).

  o Golf too became an extended interest. I think he started too late to become any good at it but enjoyed the social aspect and playing the fruit machine in the clubhouse.

o Dad's final interest – almost an obsession – was pottery. I think it started as an offshoot of his teaching – using local clay with the kids to make little pots and figures of animals, which he tried (and failed) to fire in the classroom stove. This progressed into buying proper clay from Stoke-on-Trent, installing a kiln at school, and finally, buying, for £25, a semi-derelict end-of-terrace house in Llŷn Street which he fitted out with two kilns, a potter's wheel, storage for clay and shelving for pots in the various stages of production. This was with a view to starting a late career as a potter after his retirement. As the day approached (pencilled in for Easter, 1975) he started taking samples of his work around shops throughout north Wales, building up a list of outlets which would accept his pots on sale or return. He'd also started up a popular pottery course in town. He was really looking forward to retirement after forty years as Head of Penlleiniau. Then, six months before the great day, he died of a heart attack.

Sometimes life really is a bitch.

Postscript

Comments yielded a crop of other pastimes that kept Pwllheli adults occupied:

- Old Time Dancing at the Legion Hall on Fridays.
- Whist drives in various venues.
- Radiograms – hugely ornate and impressive pieces of furniture which provided the delights of radio and gramophone records.
- Libraries – both the free public library run by the council and subscription libraries, one of which operated from W.H. Smith's.

An exchange of comments about the golf club's Manchester

Cup led to discussion about who could compete for it. One suggestion was that it was a ladies' cup, which, since one year my father won it, led me to speculate that he must have played in drag.

It's interesting to see the way discussions on Facebook wander off subject, just as they do in real life.

Smiling at the past

I often find myself smiling indulgently at how primitive things were in the past. Then on reflection I realise that the very things that I regard as primitive were in fact a great improvement on what had gone before.

- Coal was delivered to our house via a removable front step. This great slab of slate was slid to one side, and the coal thunderously emptied down a chute into the cellar. Primitive maybe, but it beat carrying filthy sacks of coal through the house, which is how it would have been done in earlier times. Scuttles-full of coal were then lifted, as needed, up the cellar steps and placed next to the kitchen range by a sophisticated piece of equipment. Me.

- Paraffin for the room heaters was delivered from the ironmongers in Gaol Street (West End Stores) by the same sophisticated piece of equipment. I'm nothing if not adaptable.

- Hot water in the house was provided by a 'back boiler' sitting behind the range in the kitchen. This was fine in winter, when the fire was roaring away all day, every day. But during the summers 'bath day' (always a Saturday) would be a fiery, steamy hell. Still better, though, than boiling endless kettles of water and filling a tin bath in front of the fire, or wrestling with a copper in an outhouse.

- Also in the kitchen was a gas light, the last survivor retained when the house was wired for electricity. During the frequent power cuts as the national grid was finding its feet, at least we had one light to fall back on. When the gas lights were first installed throughout the house, they must have been a huge improvement on faffing about with oil lamps and candles.

- Whilst Mum's first washing machine would now belong in a museum – a huge contraption with an alternating central paddle and a frighteningly powerful external mangle – it was a marvel compared with the complicated wash-day routines of my grandmother's time, with outhouse coppers, dolly-pegs, washboards and huge blocks of Sunlight soap.

- A green kitchen cupboard with a flower-like ventilator was designed to keep food cool. But it was rubbish – in the summer, pop was warm, butter turned rancid and milk went off. It was no substitute for the cool tiled dairies and pantries of the past, but, hey, those were the preserve of the rich and their big country houses. So let's hear it for the modern fridge!

- Our first TV was a hoot – a wooden cabinet with a tiny bulbous screen, across which ghostly shapes flitted and which suffered a snowstorm every time a car went up or down Llŷn Street. But still a thing of wonder, and surely better than singing around the piano. The first programme I saw on our nine-inch Cosser was an outside broadcast from the Farnborough Air show, with a commentary by Raymond Baxter. It's funny the things you remember!

- I received my first cash machine card in the very early 1970s. It was made of grey plastic, punctured with a pattern of slots. I could put this into the hole-in-the-wall machine, and it would give me £10. No more, no less. The card would be retained, and I would get it back, by post, days later. Hilarious now, but imagine – you could get money out of your account when the bank was shut!

- When Dad was planning a trip to, say, south Wales, he would write off to the AA who would send him, in a week or two, a detailed written route and map. Behold your ancestor, Google Maps! Eat your heart out Satnav!

We smile at the past, and no doubt the future will smile at us – my grandchildren are already doing it. US astronauts got to the moon with less computer-power than you now get in a singing greetings card. That's funny!

But, hey, they did get to the moon!

Postscript

Comments led to a number of reflections.

- When we think about the houses we grew up in, it's a bit like one of those 3-D postcards they used to sell, with photos taken from slightly different angles, looked at through a special viewer. The three dimensions were length, breadth, and depth. In this case, the three dimensions are in time, not space: the way it was when we were growing up, the implied way it must have been before, and the way things are today.

- Another perspective offered by the comments was the difference between Pwllheli itself and the villages and farms on the peninsula – places like Tyddyn Howel and Cefn Morfa, Morfa Nefyn. These comments, often beginning with four Yorkshiremen type comments like, 'You were lucky', were an eye-opener to one brought up with all the creature comforts of Pwllheli:

    o A group of houses supplied, through a one-inch water main, with a dribble of water so slow you could spend half a lifetime waiting to fill a kettle.
    o The joys of Elsan and earth toilets.
    o A complete absence of electricity.
    o Being bathed in a copper.
    o Heating by paraffin lamps, including one example that sounded positively dangerous – putting a paraffin

heater into the roof space of the house to stop the pipes freezing.

- There were a number of suspicious paeans of praise for the smell of paraffin. Was this an early precursor to glue sniffing?

- Private telephones were so rare that everybody in the surrounding area would want to use them. Sometimes this could lead to queues and the installation by the householder of coin boxes.

My father's death

Some nine years or so ago, Paul Shaw posted in 'Old Pictures of Pwllheli' a photograph of the staff of Penlleninau School taken in the early 1970s. A very happy picture which included his mum Yvonne Shaw, who taught at the school, and my dad Phil Simon, who was the Head. I don't know who took the picture, but it was a cracker, light-hearted and full of laughter. The comments included Paul's account of Dad's death, which was remarkably accurate given that he was a small boy at the time. But the picture and comments brought it all back, and I thought I'd add my own memories. If this post is inappropriately personal, I apologise.

In 1974 I lived in Ipswich, was a keen supporter of its football club, and had a season ticket at Portman Road. On that day, 21 September, I arrived home from the match feeling jubilant – Town had beaten Chelsea 2–0. The phone rang. It was my Uncle Owen, calling from north Wales to say that my father had died. Stunned by this bolt from the blue – he was only sixty-four, with no recent illness, no history of heart trouble – I didn't notice whilst I was on the phone what my two-year-old son was doing. I was then a pipe-smoker, and in the past I'd seen him watching carefully as I dipped the bowl of my pipe into my tobacco pouch, scooped St Bruno into it with my forefinger, tamped it down, then thrust the pipe-stem into my mouth. He was now gravely copying these actions, but with a tub of Lurpak instead of the tobacco pouch.

My father was dead; my pipe was full of butter. Life is full of tragedy and comedy, juxtaposed.

When we got to Pwllheli the next day, my distraught mother told us what had happened. Dad was going to watch a north Wales XV play a touring Tongan side in Rhyl, so they'd decided to make a day of it. They would drive to Llandudno Junction where they had friends, Mum would stay there for the afternoon, and Dad would carry on to the match. I think he also intended to visit possible outlets for his post-retirement pottery. One of the car's tyres had a slow puncture, so when they arrived in Llandudno Junction, having said their hellos, Dad got going with the foot pump whilst Mum helped the lady of the house make tea.

With the tyre pumped up Dad re-entered the house and sat down in the front room. Mum brought in his cup of tea and asked him where he wanted it. He nodded to the table next to his chair. In Mum's words, 'I put the cup and saucer down, looked up and knew straight away that he was gone.'

The funeral was delayed – since Dad had died away from home, there had to be a post-mortem. During that week my brother Jeff and I were kept busy – helping Mum with the 'arrangements' and with hosting the family (mainly her siblings) and friends, arriving to pay their respects. In Bangor, a solicitor told us the result of the autopsy ('myocardial infarction' then, seeing our incomprehension, 'heart attack'). She told us that, according to the coroner, Dad had had several minor heart attacks before, without knowing it. That was, we realised, why he was always chewing indigestion tablets.

Over the following week Jeff and I talked endlessly, trying to get to grips with his death. In a variety of pub gardens (the weather was lovely), we mulled over childhood memories. But they were all domestic memories, of Phil Simon as our father. So the great outpouring of genuine grief in Pwllheli, the packed church at his funeral, the long obituary and the poem about him in the *Caernarfon and Denbigh Herald*, the conversations in pubs around the town which started with, 'If you're half the man your father was...', took us totally by surprise.

Dad was from a working-class family in the Rhondda. After he qualified as a teacher, he worked in London for a year. Then, as I understand it, Bangor diocese, needing to appoint a primary head who could also play the organ at St Peters, contacted Trinity College Carmarthen. The college said that the only one of their alumni that fitted the bill was young Phil Simon. So, in 1934, at the age of twenty-four, Dad was appointed headteacher of Penlleiniau. An interview, apparently, was not required. When he died he'd been there for forty years, and had just started teaching the grandchildren of kids he taught when he first arrived in Pwllheli.

Postscript

Reading Paul's post brought home to me something I'd never considered before. Penlleiniau, not long after the start of the autumn term, must have closed on the Friday for a normal weekend. But on the Monday the teaching staff – Mrs Gardiner, Miss Jones, Yvonne – were faced with having to tell the kids that Mr Simon was dead. I can't imagine what that must have been like.

My daughter never knew her grandfather – she was born six months before he died. But now, at forty-seven, having seen the photograph (and others) on Facebook, having read all the comments, she told me that it had made her realise how affectionately her Taid was regarded in Pwllheli, and what a considerable figure he was in the town.

So heartfelt thanks, Paul, and all those who posted comments and memories!

CHAPTER 6

School

A FURTHER MAJOR influence on our growing is, of course, the schools we attended. Many kids whose parents move around a lot end up with memories of lots of schools, making recalling them all extremely complicated. In my case this was not so. My primary school was Penlleiniau, one of only two in the town – the other being Troed-yr-Allt. My secondary was the grammar school – Ysgol Ramadeg Pwllheli (YRP as it appeared on the school badge), widely known as 'County', again one of only two in the town – the other being the secondary modern, Frondeg, widely known as 'Central'.

Penlleiniau

My memories of Penlleiniau Primary School were complicated by the fact that my father was the Head, though the only real disadvantage of being the Head's son I can remember was that, when everybody else, desperate to answer a question, was shouting 'Sir, sir!' whilst hopping around with hands raised, I just had to wait until noticed. I could hardly shout, 'Dad, Dad!'

In my day there were three teachers: Mrs Gardiner, with her dark looks and striped college blazer, who taught the infants, Miss Jones, with a fierce bearing but, I suspect, a kind heart, who was in charge of the lower juniors, and Dad, who took the older kids. Most of my memories are of Dad's class, probably because they are the most recent.

For religious instruction, English and Welsh speakers were separated – I can still hear Dad saying, 'Saesneg, ymlaen' (English, onwards) (in Welsh? Why?), sending us English speakers traipsing off through the partition door at the back, across the dining room and into Miss Jones's room. (Embarrassing memory: question, 'What is a leper?' My answer, 'An animal with spots.')

Other memories. Biscuits sold at morning playtime to boost the school fund (very short-lived – parents complained that they were spoiling their children's appetite). Nature rambles. Playing football in the school yard, with Dad joining in (shades of the penalty-taking scene in *Kes*), Jimmy Jones miss-kicking in front of goal ('Jimmy's short leg,' we all agreed, was the cause). Making a model of a Canadian grain elevator out of toilet-roll tubes and sending a photograph, taken by Dad, to the company who owned it. They must have been impressed – they sent me a thank you letter and more than I needed to know about grain elevation in Saskatchewan. Doing a project about London and, when talking about it to the class, mispronouncing 'Thames' to rhyme with 'James'. A succession of exotic London Institute of Education students from Java and Sumatra doing their teaching practice in Pwllheli because it was a bilingual town.

Pupils were entrusted with certain jobs. Filling the ink wells from a large tin kept in the cupboard above the stove. Handing out the cod liver oil capsules and calcium tablets. Fetching the PE equipment (mats, hoops, beanbags) from the cupboard in the air-raid shelter between Dad and Mrs Gardiner's classrooms. Most prized, though, was ringing the bell – hand-held, with, on reflection, a rather grisly handle made of a goat's foot.

Becoming a headteacher myself in later years, I didn't envy Dad's gruelling full-time teaching commitment and share of playground duties. But I did envy his lack of a telephone, and, above all, his place in the community.

Postscript

The post about Penlleiniau led to a flood of memories, all positive, about this little (three teachers, including my father, the head) Church of Wales school. Some were incredibly detailed:

- Miss Jones, with a V for Victory hairstyle, would, on arrival in the morning, change into shoes with tassels, and a housecoat.

- The goat's foot bell, which trusted senior pupils were allowed to ring to fetch kids in from the playground, had to be held in a certain way, otherwise the clapper would fail to make contact with the side of the bell and would, instead, deliver a stinging blow to the wrist.

- Remembered equipment included an archaic copying machine, a guillotine which pupils were allowed to use (even under supervision, that seems a bit foolhardy) and a kiln and potter's wheel (introduced long after I'd left).

- After my time, too, were trips to London and to football matches in Manchester. We had to be satisfied with Black Rock and Tre'r Ceiri.

- Staff were held in high regard – 'Parch mawr at yr athrawon i gyd' 'Great respect to all the teachers' – even if my father, in addition to being much loved, was also feared.

- Unplanned nature rambles would be embarked upon without any talk of risk-assessments or parental permission slips – those were more innocent and less litigious times. One such nature ramble, described in considerable detail by Paul Shaw, whose mother taught at Penlleiniau, though after my time, was particularly poignant. The class walked down the hill from school, along North Street, and up into Allt Bartu, finally stopping near the cemetery at a cottage that was up for sale. With hindsight, he suspected that his mum had had an ulterior motive for the route she chose – within three months, she and his dad had bought the cottage. Indeed, they live there still. The poignancy arose from the dates. When the ramble took place, in July 1974, my father was Head of the school. By the time the family moved into the cottage three months later, he was dead.

Hobnailed boots

In school photographs taken in the 1950s, we kids look like something out of the Great Depression. Though, come to think of it, when I started school as a three year old in 1949 it was only twenty years since the Wall Street Crash sparked off the Great Depression, and only ten years since the approach of the Second World War ended it. So perhaps the way we looked is not that surprising.

The boys had hair cut in severe short-back-and-sides, wore scruffy grey shirts, home-knitted cardigans, long flannel shorts, knee-length woollen socks and hobnailed boots. I honestly can't remember what the girls looked like – I wasn't that interested. Dresses, presumably, since I do remember them tucked into their knickers when they were doing handstands against the toilet wall in Miss Jones's yard. And no short-back-and-sides.

Apart from our clean, cherubic faces we could all – girls and boys – have been on one of those street photographs taken to illustrate inner city deprivation in the slums of Liverpool or Manchester. But this post is not about our clothes in general, or how hard things were when we were young. It's about the boots.

Let me be clear. We're not talking fashionable modern hobnailed boots like those being advertised by Dolce & Gabbana for £975 which came up when I googled to check whether it was 'hobnail' or 'hobnailed' boots. Ours were cheap, no-nonsense leather footwear into which hobnails and steel tips had, to make them longer lasting, been hammered by our dads. The sort that Lonnie Donegan's dustman old man called 'daisy roots' because he had such a job pulling them up.

These boots, which we all wore, were the source of one of our greatest pleasures. It went like this.

Penlleiniau Primary School was halfway up a steep hill called Salem Terrace. When you'd been let out at half past three, you'd squat down in the middle of the road outside the school (not much traffic in those days) and friends would stand either side of you and grab your hands. They would then drag you down the hill as fast as they could run. This in itself was exciting, but the point was not just the swoop down the hill, but the great plume of sparks that poured out from your boots behind you. You were like a water-skier, being pulled by two speedboats, throwing up a crackling fiery wake.

Then, when you reached the bottom, you'd traipse back up the hill, so that somebody else could have a go.

This was not, it's true, why our mothers had bought the boots, nor why our fathers had hammered in the hobnails. But it was really, really good fun.

If you decide to try this yourselves (and here I have to admit to a smile at the picture of elderly men and women being dragged down Salem Terrace in hobnailed boots), two words of warning.

Don't touch the hobnails immediately after your go – they become red hot. And even when they're cold, be careful – they're often worn down into tiny razor-edged metal blades which can give you a nasty cut.

Postscript

The post released an unexpected flood of footwear memories, some from before my time (Ammo boots), but mainly from later. Those getting honourable mentions included:

- Chelsea boots (with zip at the side).
- Wayfinders (with animal outlines on the sole and a compass set into the heel).

- Plimsolls (also known as pumps or, to my south Walian parents, daps).
- Booties (for younger kids).
- Wellies.
- T-bar shoes (whatever they were).
- Flip-flops.
- Plastic sandals (very sweaty, but useful in the sea).
- Slip-ons.
- Brogues.
- Hush Puppies.
- Clogs (made to measure).
- Dr Scholl sandals (with wooden soles).
- Suede and cork platforms.
- Brothel-creepers (generic term for any suede shoes with crepe soles).

Many of these were illustrated with photographs. Who knew that footwear would provide such a fund of nostalgia!

Other discussion included the range of shoe shops in Pwllheli, the fact (unsuspected by me) that hobnailed boots, in the eyes of kids, conferred street-cred on their wearers, whilst in the eyes of aspiring middle-class adults were viewed, with superior disdain, as the preserve of the working class.

A description of second-hand plimsols being handed out in a village school at the start of the academic year led to horror-filled disgust on grounds of health, and this in turn provoked further comment on the spread of fungus, verrucas, herpes. Even VD was remarked upon, though not, I think, from plimsolls.

Mention was made also of the tramp of men in their 'sgidia' hoelion mawr' (hobnailed boots) on their way to work in Trefor quarry, which reminded me of the sound of miners responding to the early morning pit hooter in Ferndale.

Starting at Ysgol Ramadeg Pwllheli

I feel so sorry for kids getting ready to start secondary school in September 2020. At any time it's stressful, but this year, with Covid making sure that there would be no chance at primary school to share their fears and no secondary school visits to ease them in, it must be purgatory.

I started at YRP in September 1957:

- First there were the new clothes. Bottle green blazer with yellow breast-pocket badge. Belted gabardine mackintosh. Grey flannel shorts. New shoes, with dire warnings not to play football in them. My blazer was two sizes too big so that I could 'grow into it'. Huge shoulders, and a hem down to my knees. I quite liked it – a bit like a Teddy Boy's drape jacket. Caps with a small badge were part of the uniform, but an endangered species even among first years. The only time I can remember seeing one in the wild was when, in the sixth form, Endaf Emlyn came to school with his tiny cap perched ridiculously on top of his thatch of blond hair. He did it just to annoy the Head. ER couldn't complain – it was, after all, part of the official school uniform.

- Then there was the equipment. Platignum fountain pen. Bottle of royal blue Quink, Lakeland coloured pencils (later replaced by Conté pencils, a source of embarrassment in a Welsh school). And an Oxford geometry set consisting of a protractor, set squares, ruler, pencil sharpener, rubber, compasses, dividers, and two Perspex stencils, one of letters and numbers, the other with outlines of lab equipment. The identical Oxford geometry set, now marketed as 'vintage', can still be bought (Amazon, at £6.99). All this equipment packed into my new leather satchel by my mum.

These preparations for secondary school were exciting, a rite of passage that everyone had to go through. It was part of growing up.

Not so pleasant were the worries stirred up by reports from those who'd gone before:

- Being thrown into beds of nettles.
- Having your head stuck down the toilet.
- Horror tales of individual teachers.
- And, of course, the fear of getting lost during the upheavals of classroom changing, of having to find your way around what seemed like a huge site, of having to organise your own timetable.

In the event, it wasn't as intimidating as I'd feared. On my first day two women approached me. 'Brawd Jeffrey Simon wyt ti?' (Are you Jeffrey Simon's brother?) they enquired. Not women at all, but senior pupils, one of whom fancied my brother. It was somehow reassuring that he was there, perhaps to come to my aid if things went badly wrong. Not that he ever acknowledged me if I saw him around school.

I'd already laid my plans:

- Avoid the toilets (if the call of nature became an unignorable shout, go during lesson time when there was nobody around).
- Stay in the nettle-free centre circle of the football field.
- Draw up a tiny cardboard timetable, laminated with Sellotape, and keep it in the top pocket of my blazer.
- Stay, like a ruminant on the veldt worried about circling lions, with groups of other first years.

I soon found my feet. I hung out with children I knew from Penlleiniau. I got to know kids from Troed-yr-Allt, and from village schools from across Llŷn. I covered my textbooks and exercise books with wallpaper. And I started to spend my breaks in 'smokers' corner' between the football field and the woods, 'one of the lads' with my cigarette held between thumb and index finger, cupped by my hand.

I was now a Pwllheli Grammar School boy, learning lots of

subjects taught by specialist teachers, sometimes in labs and craft rooms full of arcane equipment. I looked back at primary school with contempt – kids' stuff. And I looked forward to freezing the blood of next year's intake with time-hallowed myths, and patronising them when they arrived ('don't they look small!') from the lofty heights of the second year.

Teachers

We were, it seems to me, lucky in the teaching staff we had at YRP – I can't think of one that I ever felt any real animosity towards.

But this also made me think about nicknames:

A. Some teachers were simply known by their Christian names:

- Maldwyn (maths). Asked by one of the sixth formers why he'd been away, he answered, '******* diarrhoea'. Malaria, it was generally agreed, contracted during the war.
- Beryl (history). At the start of her career, she lived in digs across the road to my house, and I overheard a huge fight between her and her boyfriend as I had a smoke out of my bedroom window.
- Harry (English). Ran the rugby teams and organised trips to Cardiff internationals. Always benevolent, with a twinkle in his eye. One of my heroes.
- Mair (Welsh). Strict, but lovely.

B. Other teachers were known simply by their initials:

- TH (science).
- RR (maths).
- ER (the headteacher, also known as Boss).

C. Then there were those who were identified by their subject:

- Willie Kitch.
- Jack Wood.

D. The interesting ones, though, were known for a variety of reasons:

- Juicy (biology). Because of a recurring phrase 'D'you see?'
- Brasso (history). Colour of his hair. Another of my heroes, and elements of his style I incorporated into my own approach to teaching.
- Cama (art). Because of his long strides.
- Llew (Latin). His name was Llewelyn. In Welsh, 'lion'.
- Llewes. Married to Llew, and therefore the lioness. But totally inappropriate – she was a gentle soul, and the kids gave her hell.
- Now Squared (chemistry). His name was Owen Owen.

E. Finally, there were those whose nicknames seem to have no explanation:

- Bono (Welsh).
- Caramia (French).
- Seu (arithmetic and economics). 'I taught myself economics entirely from the *Manchester Guardian*'s financial pages.'
- Mol (biology).
- Swift (English). My all-time hero, and upon whose style, as with Brasso, I based my own during thirty years as a teacher.

Sorry if I've missed any out. But as I said earlier, I think we were lucky with our teachers. Some may, of course, disagree!

Postscript

My post about YRP teachers provoked a load of comments which told me a lot of things that I hadn't known before, and shook loose a lot of things that I had known but totally forgotten. Here they are, all mixed up together:

1. Newman: A south Walian music teacher (that is, a music

teacher from south Wales, not a teacher of south Walian music). He was a lovely guy, yet my own memories of his lessons are all embarrassing.

- When he told us to compose a sixteen-bar riff, I stuck my fingers in my ears and started to hum, trying out different tunes. When I'd written down the final crochet of my masterpiece, I resurfaced to find the whole class in fits. Newman kindly tried to spare my blushes by complimenting me on my working methods, but I was mortified.
- Again, asked to critique a piece of music he'd just played. I airily announced that it was pleasantly umbricating. He tried not to laugh. There is, of course, no such word – I meant undulating.
- And finally, knowing my parents were from south Wales, he asked me to talk to the class about the Rhondda. I launched into a furious attack on its griminess, overcrowding, even its accent. He looked really hurt, and I still cringe when I think about it. I don't know why I did it – I loved Ferndale. There are downsides to being a smart-arse.

2. Mol: Mol's nickname, I learned, came from 'molars' (i.e. back teeth), pronounced in his very heavy Welsh accent. Miscellaneous memories.

- His noted expressions were 'a rare specimen', 'when I was in the army,' 'car bach yn mynd fatha wennol' (little car going like a swallow). My favourite, and one I'd not heard before, was, on the process of identifying a species of fly, 'Only the experts know,' – heavy pause whilst looking around the class – 'and I know.'
- Mol's idea of heaven was Cors Geirch, as far as I know just a marsh, but I'm sure full of wildlife.
- Mol played in goal during staff hockey matches – a substantial figure, he must have been difficult to get past.

3. Juicy:
   - Whilst invigilating, Juicy had us in fits because, sitting at the desk at the front, her little legs didn't reach the floor.
4. Maldwyn:
   - Maldwyn, in his own free time, taught chess to anyone who was interested.
   - He had several stock expressions, including 'hen gwcw' (old cuckoo), 'hen gloman' (old dove) and 'gloman wirion' (silly dove).
5. Swift:
   - Swift was, I learned, so called because of his similarity to Man City goalkeeper Frank Swift.
   - He could often be seen wandering around Pwllheli after school because he'd forgotten where he'd parked his car.
   - At one point, apparently, he had for several weeks unknowingly hauled around in his ever-present rucksack a shot put placed there as a joke by other members of staff.
   - Highly intelligent and sensitive, an excellent sportsman who joined the medical corps rather than a fighting unit during the war, it's Swift I think about when the term 'Alpha Male' comes up.

Reminiscing about school is of course time sensitive. When I was at YRP, certain teachers were coming towards the end of their careers – I particularly enjoyed head of science TH being likened in looks to Lee Van Cleef. Other teachers were just establishing themselves as I left – Keith, for example, and Bethan Ogwen. Yet others came after I left, so I know nothing about them – Fred Bloggs, Dave Roberts, Boi Geog, Auntie Marilyn. But don't you love the names!

Finally, three stories that made me laugh out loud, and surely worth preserving for posterity:

- Two girls being 'knuckled' by Caramia as they talked behind their uplifted desks at the front of the class. The lesson they learned? Not, as you might expect, to stop talking in class, or even to avoid being caught, but, from then on, always to sit at the back.

- A group of girls peering up Bono's sleeve to count how many layers of clothing he had on. Disturbing this one, in so many ways.

- Two girls in the physics lab, having been separated by Dic Ed for talking and therefore sitting on opposite side-benches, slowly inching their stools backwards and then around, to meet on the back bench and continue their conversation.

As one of the oldest members of this group, and also myself a retired teacher, I read the comments, especially the ones about teachers of whom I'd never heard, with that feeling of panic when the class is getting away from you. 'OMG', I thought, 'They're talking amongst themselves!'

But that's a good thing, right?

Brasso

In my last post I mentioned Brasso, one of my favourite teachers at YRP. A few memories:

- He was responsible for my first published writing, when I was sixteen – a book review in the first edition of the school history magazine.

- Apart from A-Level history, Brasso also taught the 'economic history' element of A-Level economics (Seu covered the economic theory element). Brasso had been talking about the Government's response to 'a run on the banks' – people withdrawing all their money, threatening the banks with collapse and causing a major economic downturn. I'd not been listening, and when he asked me how the government dealt with the problem, I blurted out that they'd organised a sports day on the banks of the Thames. His face was a picture.

- Another time, going over one of my essays, he said that he liked the fact that I didn't use big words just for the sake of it. I didn't like to own up that this was because I didn't know any big words.

- As part of our A-Level history course he took us to Bangor University to attend a lecture by world-famous historian Christopher Hill. Although the content of the lecture was excellent, it was delivered in a flat, boring monotone, not improved by a severe stutter. Brasso was sitting next to me, and I eventually turned to him to see what he thought of it. He was fast asleep.

- The last time I saw Brasso was on the day that the A-Level results came out. Tony Pierce had a car, and we drove around several of our teachers to thank them for their hard work. Brasso's house was down a lane off the Pwllheli to Cricieth road. He came out of a comfortably disorganised kitchen and took us into a beautiful lounge. He congratulated us on our results, but with a slightly distracted air – he'd forgotten it was results day. Brasso's house – on a leafy lane, big lived-in farmhouse kitchen, posh lounge for visitors – has been my ideal template ever since, though I've never managed to replicate it.

Postscript

The response to the post about Brasso served to emphasise something which I didn't realise at the time: that I knew virtually nothing about the private lives of my teachers. It gave tantalising glimpses, no more, of the life he led outside school:

- At some point he lived in Glancymerau, during which time he was described as 'a true gentleman' who 'battled his illness with dignity'.

147

- At another point in his life he shared a flat in the West End with the late husband of one of the group members. His daughter remembers that time as being great fun, with most of each day being spent on the beach.

- Another group member recalls babysitting for that daughter.

- A picture exists of him showing a pupil how to pour beer from a bottle without creating too much of a head. In Greece. At 9am. A school trip possibly? Seems unlikely, but I don't know. A man after my own heart, though.

- Another post had RIP added to his name. No surprise – I suppose he would have been into his nineties by now. Yet it still came as a shock.

- Finally, one comment included a picture of the front page of a paper he'd written. Titled '1775 – The Royal Welsh Fusiliers in Boston, by Gwynfor Jones, MA', it was published in the 1978 *Transactions of the Honourable Society of Cymmrodorion*. A little research revealed that this was (and is) a London-based Welsh scholarly society first established in 1751 whose *Transactions* have been published regularly since 1897, and which played an important part in the setting up of the National Eisteddfod, Aberystwyth University, and the National Museum and National Library of Wales. No further proof needed, then, of his historical 'chops'.

I know nothing further of his life. I'm sorry he had to battle illness. I wonder why he lived in Glancymerau and the West End instead of that lovely farmhouse somewhere between Pwllheli and Cricieth. I can only assume that this was the result of some sort of family breakdown. I don't know why he gave a beer-pouring tutorial on a Greek morning, though I'm glad that he did.

He was a lovely man whose influence lives on in me, no doubt too in hundreds of his other pupils, and possibly, in a sort of cascade effect, even in pupils that I myself have taught. What greater accolade could any teacher hope for.

The curse of the severed hand

Even if you're not superstitious, at the back of your mind there might still be an uneasy thought that the dead can reach out from beyond the grave and punish you for disrespecting them. This was brought home to me in Mol's lab in the New Block, whilst we were waiting for our O-Level Biology lesson to begin.

On a shelf at the back, a group of us found a skeletal hand. It was there, no doubt, to show how the bones of the hand related to each other, and how they were articulated. As a visual aid, you'd have to agree that it did its job – I can still name the bones (the carpals, metacarpals and phalanges) nearly sixty year later.

They were, I think, genuine bones, not plastic replicas, and as such really should have been treated with reverence. They were threaded onto stout wire, bent at the tips of the fingers and thumb to stop them falling off. And they were, of course, a gift to any idiot intent on raising a laugh in class.

Yes, I was that idiot. I grabbed the skeletal hand, pulled down the sleeve of my school blazer to cover my fist, and started chasing other members of the class, trying to stroke their hair, steal their pens and worse. Everybody scattered, screaming with laughter.

As things were quietening down, I raised my game. I manipulated the bony hand until the index finger was standing proud of the rest, then poked it up my right nostril. This brought about further outbreaks of hysterics.

That's when things went wrong.

I felt a sharp pain deep inside my nose, and blood started to trickle out. The bent wire, sharp as the barb on a fishhook, had embedded itself in my nasal cavity. The more I pulled, the deeper in it went and the more it hurt. The trickle of blood became a stream. The rest of the class tried to look sympathetic, without much success. I stood before them, the skeletal hand hanging from my nostril, blood flooding down its index finger. To complete my humiliation, my eyes started watering copiously, and tears poured down my face.

At this point, Mol walked in and set about restoring order. As he did so, I ducked down behind the rear bench and finally managed to rip the dead hand out of my nose. I stuck it (the hand, not my nose) back on the shelf then, running a gauntlet of barely suppressed giggling, walked to the front and told Mol that I was having a nosebleed, something he could quite clearly see for himself. He sent me to Willie Kitch to be treated. As I walked across the yard to the domestic science room, I wondered what the next person to encounter the bony hand would make of it being covered in blood.

The threefold moral of the story is clear. Don't mess about in class. Don't pick your nose.

But above all, don't disrespect the dead.

Postscript

This post provoked a number of memorable comments:

- My brother pointed out that after I'd left Pwllheli, well into my forties, I was plagued by quite serious nosebleeds, several of which led to my being hospitalised. Could this, he asked, be 'the curse of the severed hand'? OMG, I thought, I hadn't made the connection! It must be true – just think of Lord Caernarfon and the Valley of the Kings! So I immediately changed the title of the post.

- A teacher member of the group looked back to a school which had been home to a human skull. Not only that, but it was, allegedly, that of a murderer called 'Yr Hwntw Mawr'. This in turn led to the helpful provision by a member of the group of a link to a Wikipedia entry about the very same. He was, apparently, a man called Thomas Edwards, an itinerant workman who'd been employed at different times in the Parys Mountain copper mines on Anglesey and as a labourer on repairs to the Cob in Porthmadog. Whilst involved in the latter, he heard rumours of a hoard of money hidden in a farm near Portmeirion. Entering the farmhouse with nefarious intent, he was disturbed by Mary Jones, the eighteen-year-old maid of the house, who was preparing food for the family. He stabbed her with a pair of shears. He made his escape, pursued by a group of local men. Eventually caught (but not before an uncle of the victim, during the pursuit, had drowned trying to cross the River Dwyryd), he was tried in Bala and executed in Dolgellau. The body of Mary Jones is buried in the churchyard at Llanfrothen. Since the Wikipedia entry is in Welsh, which is not my first language, I apologise if this account is inaccurate. If not totally wrong.

- Another story was of Robat Jones, a farmer in Trefor, being bamboozled by his two sons. I won't go into detail, but it involved the progressive inflation of a deceased piglet. Not much to do in 1940s Trefor, apparently.

School assemblies

It has to be said that school assemblies at YRP weren't much fun. Not only were they boring, but you didn't even get to sit down. It was, however, sometimes possible to wring a few laughs out of them.

- ER held his investigative skills in high regard, often comparing himself to Inspector Maigret. One morning he was having a rant about the vandalising of the boys' toilets. During it he signalled to a prefect in the wings who, looking sheepish, struggled across the stage carrying a large cast-iron cistern lid. The result was, inevitably, the slow spread of muted giggling, starting among the senior pupils at the back. This was not at all the response he was looking for. Turning a delicate shade of pink, he said with suppressed fury, 'Hold it by the edges, there might be fingerprints.' The giggling turned to helpless laughter which spread through the hall. Deciding to cut his losses, with a swirl of his cape ER stalked off the stage.

- On occasion a strange phenomenon could be observed in assembly. Normally we were packed into the hall relatively tightly, like wheat in a field. But sometimes a wide crop-circle empty of pupils would appear, with just one person standing at its centre. Depending on character, this person would either be looking embarrassed, or grinning widely. The explanation was of course that the person in the centre had 'dropped one'.

- As part of our duties, we prefects had to do readings from the stage during assembly. As Tony Pierce's turn on the rota approached, he warned us to pay close attention to his declamatory style, but when we pressed him for further details he would say no more. The morning arrived, his reading began – a story from the New Testament. We looked at each other questioningly – the reading seemed perfectly normal. Then, with the first mention of Jesus Christ, all became clear. He pronounced it in such a way, with such controlled vehemence, that it sounded like an expletive. It was finely judged – not obvious enough to alert Boss but clear enough to set those in the know sniggering. Childish, I know, but you have to take your pleasures where you find them.

Postscript

Some interesting facts and stories arose from the post about YRP assemblies:

The tradition of prefects doing readings in assemblies pierced the hearts of most of us with abject terror, to the extent that one prefect, adept at the arts of public speaking from long experience at his local chapel, was happy to take on this onerous task from others, presumably in return for a small fee. Other more outgoing souls would use their moment of fame on stage to wind up the powers that be. One, it is said, chose as his text the shortest verse in the Bible, which he spat out as an expletive rather than as a catalyst for religious thought. 'Jesus wept!' Another omitted the final 'Amen', so that it came out, not as 'For Christ's sake, Amen – pause – 'please sit', but as, 'For Christ's sake, sit!' Yet another chose as his text the longest Bible reading possible (the 'begats' perhaps), the mumbling through of which caused Boss to become increasingly apoplectic until he could finally stand it no longer and rudely interrupted the lesson to continue the assembly. (How this all squares with the readings actually being chosen by RE teacher Stan I've no idea.)

Another source of amusement in assemblies was Boss's penchant for over-dramatic forensic claims. For example, after a malicious setting off of the fire alarms, he claimed portentously that he would be sending for the CID to fingerprint the glass of the alarm if the culprit didn't immediately appear at his office. The culprit didn't turn up, and neither did the CID.

It was interesting to note that assemblies didn't change at all between when I was at school and when my younger brother attended twelve years later, prompting my brother's question, 'How could Boss be in school for all that time and learn nothing?'

Rugby

At YRP in the 1960s we were given a choice of football or rugby. My friends and I chose rugby. Two reasons – several of us had older brothers who were in the first XV, and Wales were a major force in international rugby. In football, not so much.

Facilities were not brilliant. For a while we played on the main football field in school and changed in a corrugated iron shed that had been condemned by the inspectors' reports in the Blue Books of 1847. There were two big iron baths, served by freezing cold water turned brown by rust. Then we had our own pitch in the West End – a mile or so walk from town, with the chance of sloping off for a fag. We changed in a derelict red-brick building next to the pitch.

The driving force behind rugby at school was Harry Hughes – he organised trips each year to Cardiff Arms Park for internationals, would let us watch matches at his bungalow next to the school, would turn a blind eye to smoking at the back of the bus on the way to away fixtures, and also to our war chant on driving into the away school car park: 'We are the boys who make most noise.' Doing press-ups on the top field during training, all puffing and panting, he shouted, 'Every little Woodbine is now rearing its ugly head!' And he told the story of one of his own teachers who would ask a boy, 'What shape's a football?', and if the answer was 'round', would clip him around the ear.

Seeing Pwllheli today with its flourishing rugby club (is it true that George North played here as a junior?), I feel proud that we had a small part in the rooting of the game in this part of north Wales. Maximum respect, as they say, to Harry Hughes and those early school rugby teams.

School routines

It's easy to remember the stand-out highlights of attending school at YRP. The regular routines are more elusive.

At the start of the academic year you got new textbooks and covered them – with brown paper, leftover gift-wrap, or even wallpaper. Exercise books also had to have your name and form on. One exercise book per subject, plus a rough book. When you got to O- and A-Level, it was useful to number successive exercise books, and even write a list of contents on the front cover. Or was it just swats like me that did that?

The daily routine started with the steep climb up Salem Terrace. After getting through the narrow gate, climbing the steps and walking up the drive, it was off to smokers' corner at the far, right-hand side of the field, where it started to slope down towards Allt Bartu. Further cigarette visits took place during morning and afternoon break. Dinner time would depend on where you ate – I went home, so could spend my spare time sitting in Brexo, walking around town or playing snooker in the Conservative Club.

At the end of each term there were exams. We'd all stand outside our allocated rooms, those of us who took them seriously (and I was one of them) mumbling and with a faraway look in our eyes as we mentally went over what we'd been learning. Each room would contain pupils from two different years, so that, theoretically, we couldn't help each other. I remember nudging the second year sitting next to me and whispering that the yoke of an egg is *yellow*, not blue. I also remember Brasso rushing in at the last minute with our history papers, hot off the press. We were all sure, because of the smell of alcohol, that he'd been to the pub at lunchtime. It wasn't until recently that I twigged. To quote Wikipedia, 'The faintly sweet aroma of pages fresh off the duplicator was a feature of school life in the spirit-duplicator era.' Abject apologies, then, to Brasso for suspecting him of lunchtime boozing.

Exam scripts were returned during normal lessons, handed back in descending order, and in public. Great if you were near the top, but if you were near the bottom, not so much. Talk about the walk of shame.

Then, at the end of term, school would close early and we'd all head for Brexo. We'd open our reports (the envelope was addressed to parents, but a sneak preview was essential for preparing responses to parents' responses), and wallow in the prospect of no school for several weeks.

At the end of the summer term there was school sports day and then the County Sports in Bangor. My last county sports day was both a triumph and a disaster. I was, I'm proud to announce, a quarter of the Caernarfonshire four times hundred and ten-yard junior relay champions. On the other hand, I have to admit that, in the individual hundred-yard hurdles, I came last, having tripped on the first hurdle and fallen flat on my face.

Back at YRP, the main school sports teams would play each other. One year our rugby team beat the football team at football and the hockey team at hockey, though I'm sure any surviving members of those humbled squads will deny it. And yes, we beat the hockey team, but we all swore we'd never play hockey again. Our opponents were the spawn of St Trinian's, the Bash Street Kids and Vlad the Impaler, all rolled into one, and the sport, we discovered, is not only more violent than rugby, but has the addition of sticks as lethal weapons.

My only other abiding memory of the day-to-day experience of being at YRP was the relentless school-uniform warfare between kids and the Head. For the girls this seemed to centre on skirt length. Girls would leave home the picture of modesty with skirts below the knee, then, as they climbed the hill to school, waistbands would be rolled and the hemlines would crank upwards. For us boys, the main battlegrounds were shoes (no crepe-soled suede brothel-creepers) trouser width (drainpipes were a no-no), and ties (to be worn with top shirt button done up). I can remember Tony Pierce, his shirt open and his tie askew, being told by ER that he looked like 'a browned-off American reporter'.

The other perpetual bone of contention was hair. If you deviated from the normal short back and sides, you'd attract Boss's most extreme response. In those pre-skinhead days, it was long hair that provoked the greatest ire. The older boys with their quiffs and DAs modelled on Elvis, us youngsters with our Beatles or Stones cuts, seemed to drive him beyond the reach of reason. It all seems so silly now.

And finally, a few words about parents' evenings.

There weren't any.

Postscript

Most of the memories of school routines shaken loose by this post involved hairstyles or school uniform:

- As evidenced by the comments, there can't have been many fifth or sixth formers who hadn't, at some point, been told to get their hair cut. Disguising its length by pushing it behind the ears seemed to have little effect on the persecution.

- Sideburns were also banned. A member of a family not noted for its adherence to the rules (oh alright, the Martins) was told to shave his off with the gibe, 'Who do you think you are, boy? Harry Secombe?'

- Girls were not immune either from the hair police. One was chased by Boss wielding a hairbrush, intent on sorting out her fashionably back-combed beehive.

- The main sartorial cause of friction between us boys and the Head seemed to be drainpipes – trousers with a width of less than fourteen inches. During my brother's time (some twelve years later) it was flares. ('You look as if you belong to the Canadian Navy!' Why 'Canadian' is anybody's guess.)

- One girl was told off for wearing a headscarf on the way up the hill to school during a cloudburst. What on earth could be wrong with that, I hear you ask. It was red, and therefore not in school colours.

- Another girl was hauled off the hockey field and dragged to Boss's office for some minor misdemeanour. She was still in her hockey shorts. Imagine the tabloid headlines if that happened today!

- A final cause of child/Boss friction was over what food the kitchens could serve. Specifically, chips. Boss was dead set against allowing chips onto the menu, no-one knows why. He probably thought that chips would lead to a decline in overall standards. Or perhaps he'd read that they didn't allow chips at Eton. In due course, like King Canute, he was overwhelmed by the tide, and, to his credit, and to universal approval from the pupils and I suspect most of the staff, chips were allowed.

- One other comment provided welcome confirmation of something that had preyed on my mind for fifty years. Hockey is a ferociously dangerous game fit only for homicidal maniacs. All the footballers and rugby players, it seems, agreed that, in the end-of-year inter-team matches, it was the one against the hockey team that was most feared. I was so relieved to discover that it wasn't just me being a wimp. Yey!

Boss – an anecdote

There have been several mentions of the Boss/ER in recent posts. Most have been negative and I can sympathise with that – I was caned twice (three strokes for offering silly excuses, six for smoking). But, canings apart, he was always perfectly nice to me, and Tony Pierce surprised me by saying that Boss had helped him to get the college place he wanted after he'd left school (who knew!). And I've been head of two secondary schools, so I know how easy it is to be misunderstood! I thought, therefore, that I'd add an anecdote which perhaps shows him in a more favourable, more human, light.

When I was in the sixth form (or Form Six, as we called it) he fetched me out of 'prep' to help with his exam preparations. Desks having been laid out (for O-Levels, or A-Levels, or both – I can't remember), candidate numbers had to be stuck to each one. So he gave me a pot of glue and a brush, and I had to walk ahead of him, whacking a dollop of paste onto each desk as he followed behind me slapping down a square of paper with the candidate number on it.

When we'd finished, as we walked back towards his office, he called in to various rooms to talk to the teachers in charge. Whenever I got the chance, I liberally smeared any door handles nearby with glutinous gobs of glue. (alliteration – Swift would have been proud!) Childish, I know, but at the time it seemed a bit of a wheeze. The last room he stopped at was upstairs (Room 1?), next to what was laughingly called the 'Sixth Form Common Room' – a charmless, dusty area that nobody used. As I waited, I liberally coated the room's door handle with glue. He came out of Room 1, and for reasons I've yet to fathom, grasped the handle of the Sixth Form Common Room and went in.

He came out wiping gunge off his hand, looked at me with my pot of glue and brush, and said, 'Simon, did you put glue on this handle?' To my shame, I denied it – the only time in my life I've ever lied. To his everlasting credit, he believed me.

When we got back to his office he left me at the door. However, it was ajar, and I could see into the room. He glanced around (presumably to check that his secretary wasn't around), walked over to the window, and wiped his hand on the curtains.

Being off school

Being unwell isn't much fun, but it does rather depend on how poorly you are. My own memories of the illnesses of my youth, because they weren't very serious, are actually bathed in a nostalgic glow.

When I was eight I had jaundice. The main downside of this was that I turned yellow – not only my skin, but the whites of my eyes. Given that I didn't *feel* ill, this was more than compensated for by several weeks off school and an instruction from Doctor Charles that I must eat lots of fruit. Since fruit was an exotic rarity in our house, this met with my unalloyed approval. I also felt rather special – everybody got measles and chicken pox and mumps, but I'd never heard of anybody getting yellow jaundice.

Whilst lying in my bed a feeling of transcendental calm

enveloped me, brought on by the knowledge that everybody else was in school. This was enhanced by the novelty of having a huge bowl of fruit on my bedside table, and the comforting sounds rising up from downstairs of my mother doing the housework – cooking, cleaning, hoovering, washing – whilst she sang songs which I've since encountered watching old films on the telly.

My second period off school was when I broke my leg playing rugby. It was in my first term in 'Form Six' – probably October/November 1962. Though I wouldn't have chosen for it to happen, it did at least mean that I'd miss the end-of-term exams.

When I got back from C&A in Bangor, the whole family managed, with much huffing and puffing, to drag me up the two flights of stairs to my bedroom at the top of the house. To start with I had to lie flat on my back, because the cast, which stretched from my toes to my crotch, stopped me turning on my side. My father brought our family radio up and installed it next to the bed to keep me company. He also left me a yard-long ruler, to use as a leg scratcher.

In due course my bed was moved down to the front room, partly so that I wasn't isolated upstairs, but mainly, I suspect, to save my mother having to traipse up and down two flights of stairs every time I needed something. It also allowed mates to come in to visit without having to trudge through the rest of the house. My father asked if there was anything I needed to help pass the time, so I asked for a guitar – I'd always wanted one, and my brother Jeff was being taught to play by John Prys. Instead, my father bought me a ukulele. It was blue and white, with a picture of a Mexican sitting under a tree on the front. Whilst it did little for my street-cred, I did manage to learn a load of chords which were easily transferred to the guitar when I eventually got my hands on one.

The boys visited me almost every day. During those first few weeks the school rugby team lost every fixture, and I was able to crow, to howls of derision, that it was because I wasn't playing. They soon got their own back. We were now sixteen, and it was coming up to Christmas. For the first time in our lives there were dances, parties and nights in the pub to look forward to. They brimmed with plans, gleefully rubbing in that I wouldn't be able to go to any of them. Even into the New Year, when I was up and about on crutches and a walking cast, I couldn't join in. It was a terrible winter – it even snowed heavily in Pwllheli – and I couldn't risk having a fall.

Being off school had been great, but its pleasures, by Christmas, were definitely beginning to pall.

Postscript

Remembering childhood is like watching home movies seen through the eyes of the child that you were. But the wonders of the Internet allow you, within seconds, to check what you remember against what Google says actually happened. Two examples:

1. The song I most vividly remember my mother singing as she hoovered was, 'I'll string along with you.' So I looked it up. It was recorded by Ginger Rogers and Dick Powell in 1934, as part of the musical comedy film *Twenty Million Sweethearts*. This confirms my eight-year-old's memory – it *is* a typical 1930s film song, and my mother must have first heard it when she was eighteen. So it would be like me singing Beatles songs whilst I did housework. If I ever did housework.

2. My sixteen year old's memory of the winter of 1962/63 as extremely cold and snowy is spot on. Starting in the run-up to Christmas '62, it was the coldest British winter since 1740, outstripping even the famously severe winter of 1947, with blizzards, snow drifts and temperatures below minus twenty degrees centigrade.

So let's hear it for childhood memories! And Google, of course.

School trip abroad

In the summer of 1962, when I was fifteen, I went on a Caernarfonshire Education Committee trip to Holland and Belgium. I remember virtually nothing of the castles, Second World War sites and museums that were the ostensible reasons for the trip. What I do remember was how much fun it was, and that it was educational, though perhaps not in the way the organisers intended.

Here's what I remember:

- My parents paid for the trip, but I had to provide my own pocket money. I did so by working all summer as a trolley-boy in Butlins. That's how, too, I earned enough to buy myself a kit to make the moccasins I was determined to take with me.

- We stayed in a huge hotel just off Russell Square in London. Some boys (from Penygroes) made water bombs with balloons and dropped them on passing pedestrians. We Pwllheli lads wished that we'd thought of it.

- The hostel we stayed at in Axel was modern, and very – well – Dutch. For example, the food seemed odd, the building included a lot of glass and polished wood, and the staff who ran it spoke good but peculiar English. Furthermore, the toilets were so designed that what you ejected from your body stayed coiled on a ceramic shelf until you flushed it away. This had the advantage of preventing the uncomfortable splash-back we were familiar with in Wales, but it made things considerably smellier.

- The hostel was permanently besieged by Dutch youths, hoping to get off with Welsh girls. The hostel had, as a fire escape, an internal, highly-polished central slide fed by tributary slides from the different dormitories. This would, in the event of fire, allow lightning-fast escape, though the whole system was made of wood, which seemed a bit counter-productive. We boys managed, with much suppressed giggling, to navigate these polished tunnels at night to get into the girls' dormitory.

- Initially we were allowed by the teachers to go off into the town on our own. This was probably a mistake on their part. Local bar staff seemed to have no concept of underage drinking. One of our number, an angelic little blond lad who couldn't have been older than twelve, ordered, with a cigar clamped between his teeth, a brandy. The only reaction of the barmaid was to hoot with laughter and signal to other customers to come and see. But she served him. It ended up with him being so drunk that, back in the dormitory, he leapt insanely from top bunk to top bunk until he fell catastrophically to the floor. We thought he was dead, until he started to shake with laughter. For the next few nights we were all grounded, and condemned to dancing, darts and table tennis in the hostel. 'Isn't this better?' one of the teachers asked, to a deafening silence.

- When we were next allowed out, we discovered two things in Axel – Bols gin, and a strange pub game which consisted of what looked like a half-size billiard table, but without pockets. So it was like billiards, but with no pots or in-offs, only cannons.

- On a day trip to Brussels, I entered a shop to buy a small silver pendant of the 'Manneken Pis' (a little boy urinating – odd the things that become tourist attractions). I pointed at it and asked how much it was. Shaking his head, the proprietor replied, 'No English!' and called for his daughter to translate. To pass the time before she appeared from the back of the shop, I said in my best schoolboy French, 'Il fait beau aujourd'hui'. He shook his head again. 'No English.' I was crestfallen.

- On another day trip (I don't remember where), I was sitting with a group of what were now friends from other parts of Caernarfonshire in an outdoor café, and we were talking Welsh. A patrician old lady at the next table spoke to us, trying first Dutch, then German, then French, and eventually English. Having established a common language, she asked us what language we'd been speaking. We told her. She looked interested, asked us a lot of questions, and jotted the answers down in a notebook she took out of her handbag.

- On yet another day trip, my beloved moccasins nearly got me killed. On wet castle ramparts they became incredibly slippery, and nearly deposited me into the courtyard far below.

After the holiday it was back to the real world – O-Level results (published in the *Caernarfon and Denbigh Herald* whilst we were away), then starting in Form Six. Within three months I'd broken my leg playing rugby against HMS Conway (see earlier). Within two years I was at university, living in Passfield Hall, a ten-minute walk from the hotel we'd stayed at near Russell Square.

I think that, in life, we all have lots of periods of transition, and in my life this trip was one of them.

It was nearly sixty years ago. Imagine!

Postscript

The trip I described took place in the summer of 1962. Some of the comments were from people who had been on that specific trip. Others had been on similar trips organised by the local authority, but in different years, ranging from 1959 to 1966. I racked my brains for the names of any of the places we visited, then did a bit of research. This is what I found out:

- Axel, where we stayed, is a town of around seven thousand people, making it a lot bigger than Pwllheli but a lot smaller than Caernarfon.

- Walcheren, a region, not a town, which lies at the mouth

of the Sheldt estuary, is all dunes and dykes. This rings a bell. There were major battles there in 1940 and 1944, which accounts for my faint memories of tanks retained as monuments.

- Middelburg is the capital of Walcheren. It is, apparently, a fine medieval town, but I remember nothing about it.
- Terneuzen is another town in the region. All that remains in my memory is its name.
- The Atomium, which we visited on our day trip to Brussels, is 335 feet tall and is a model of a ferrite crystal magnified 165 billion times. I don't know why. It was part of the Brussels World Fair of 1958. It's still there – I've passed it several times when driving to Greece.

Two other things I discovered from the comments:

- The large hotel we stayed at in London was the Russell Hotel. It seems to have been used on all of these trips – perhaps, someone suggested, Caelloi Motors had an agreement with them. I remember seeing, from my room, what I assumed was a cathedral. It was, I found out later, St Pancras station.
- Spaghetti Bolognese was regarded by us all as very exotic, and we didn't like the smell of parmesan which, we agreed, smelled of sick.

I suspect that such trips are now a rarity, except for children with prosperous parents. Such a shame.

Private education and the class system

Until I went away to university in England, I always thought, when I gave it any thought at all, that private education was for kids:

- Who couldn't hack it in state schools, and
- Whose parents could afford to beam them out and pay

large sums of money for an inferior education in some distant 'Dotheboyshall'.

In other words, private schools were there to relieve state schools of dim middle-class kids who were holding the rest of us back. Why else, I wondered, would such schools have the charity status which conferred on them all sorts of tax benefits, allowing the country's taxpayers to kindly contribute to the education of these poor (or rather rich) wretches?

Imagine my surprise when I got to the London School Economics, a famously left-wing college, to discover that public schools like Eton and Harrow, far from being remedial schools for the less academically-gifted scions of the nice-but-dim wealthy classes, were in fact the cornerstones of a class system, headed by the Royal family, created to ensure that the English aristocracy kept their iron grip on power, influence and above all dosh. And in perpetuity. I was astonished!

Not, I'd have to admit, that I had any experience of private education, personally or even vicariously. The only guy I ever knew in Pwllheli who went to a private school was Dafydd Bodlew, and when he suddenly disappeared to Llandovery College I thought, inasmuch as I thought about it at all, that he'd not been working hard enough at YRP and so had (possibly as a punishment) been 'sent away' to school by his parents. I have to emphasise here that this was a thoughtless assumption by the callow youth that I then was and is almost certainly totally inaccurate.

Dafydd was not noticeably dim, and his friendship came with considerable benefits. I mentioned in a previous post that he had unfettered access to a flat above his dad's veterinary practice. He also had the keys to a caravan beyond Tudweiliog where we spent a night smoking Peter Stuyvesant cigarettes and telling rude jokes. Another time we slept in a chicken shed on Caeau Gwynion Farm and went on military manoeuvres across the fields beyond. Needless to say, we were the squaddies, he was the officer – he was after all a member of Llandovery's

Officer Training Corps. We even made a war film – yes, he owned a movie camera. What I'd give to see a copy today!

It seemed to me at the time that social class wasn't an issue in Pwllheli in the 1950s and '60s, among us kids anyway. Naïve, perhaps. Might it have been that, apart from Dafydd Bodlew, I never came across the posh kids because they were all away at snooty boarding schools?

Postscript

I found the responses to my 'Private Education' post very – well – educational. They persuaded me that my own attitudes to privately-educated children were perhaps too simplistic and even a bit uncharitable.

A picture emerged of us north Wales state-school kids picking up our ideas of private education from *Mallory Towers*, *Billy Bunter* and the *Famous Five*, then experiencing real private school kids as nicer than you'd expect and more to be pitied than envied. They were separated from the love of their families for large parts of the year, and were often not that posh, but the children of squaddies or civil servants who'd been posted abroad and had no choice but to park their progeny in private schools rather than haul them around the world in their luggage. Even the posh ones, it often seemed, would have preferred to be at home, but weren't given that choice (unlike two of the commentators, both of whom flatly refused to be sent away to private school at all).

Stories emerged of bedraggled English boys from a Porthdinllaen summer camp having to order what they wanted from outside the Bay Tree Café in Morfa Nefyn whilst their snobbish, posh and portly teacher Basil ('dressed in Baden-Powell shorts'!) did the buying – according to one commentator who worked there from the age of eleven. Of another's dad in Trefor being made to wait outside the quarry manager's palatial house when he called for his friend Stephen, only for his mum to take revenge by making

Stephen wait in turn outside their two-up-two-down in the village.

Other stories were reported back by Pwllheli-ites who'd gone out into the world. A middle-class major running a moonlighting catering business using army resources, a bit like Milo Mindbender in *Catch-22*. An Ambleside encounter with 'public school chaps' to whom this Welsh-accented state-school oik was actually rather exotic. They were, though, friendly, knowledgeable and obsessed with sport – they were horrified when he told them that his school back in Pwllheli didn't have a cricket team! They considered a Pwllheli upbringing to be 'wild and exciting', and they really envied him his access to girls. I bet they did.

And though I'd been shamed by the generous attitude of some to the privately educated, I have to admit to cheering on others with less charitable comments:

- One's suspicion at an English minor public school at which he taught, that the entrance exam consisted of only two questions: 'Are you thick?' and 'Are your parents rich.'

- Another's view that private schools are, 'Hotbeds of competitive anorexia, body-shaming and bullying,' offering, not a superior education, but only 'connections'. Living in Harrow, she likened walking among its entitled pupils to 'stepping back in time'.

- And we've all seen the devastating effects on British politics in the last ten years of an Eton education which instilled confidence totally unjustified in any way by intellect or ability.

My memory that hardly any kids from Pwllheli went to private school also proved to be wide of the mark. Loads of kids did – the children of doctors, businessmen, bankers – sometimes with employers offering help with fees as a perk. There was a report of a man with a very posh accent who seemed to know a lot about Pwllheli. Turned out he was *from* Pwllheli but had always gone to private schools, and consequently had never had any dealings with us state-school lads.

There were clearly two Pwllhelis, and ours was the one that was 'below stairs'.

CHAPTER 7

On the Fringes

APART FROM FRIENDS and family, we encountered hundreds of others who lived in our home town. We're all the stars in our own lives, but one of a cast of thousands in the lives of others. Here are the ones who immediately sprang to mind.

A cast of thousands

First, some examples of people who I didn't know well but who, for one reason or another, I remember, even though it's almost certain they wouldn't remember me:

- Mike Bowie. I remember what he looked like (good-looking and cool) and where he lived (in the High Street), but the main thing that pops into my mind is – and I've no idea if it's true – that he was friends with Douglas Crocket, that they often got into trouble, and that, when dealing with the police (as they were frequently forced to do), the fact that their surnames were those of two American frontiersmen who died at the Alamo led to unfair accusations that Bowie and Crocket were not their real names, and that they were just, well, taking the piss.

- Martin Griffiths, who lived just down the road from us, and who was once bitten on the eye by a horsefly. It left him with the biggest shiner I've ever seen.

- Colin Moss – a big lad who, when he worked behind the bar at the West End, was the first person I'd come across using the word 'Cheers' instead of 'thank you'. I also have a feeling that it was at his family's prefab in Morfa'r Garreg that I first saw a television – my mother had been invited along to watch the Coronation in 1953. We kids, thank god, were allowed to play outside.

- Malcolm Goodfellow. I remember what he looked like, and that he lived in Ffordd-y-Maer. But otherwise it's a blank – I don't think our paths ever really crossed. But what a memorable name!

- Ronald Redfern. By far the best footballer of his generation.

- The Matthews family. I knew the boy, but most worthy of note were his albinistic sisters who reputedly sold their beautiful pure white hair to wigmakers for impressive sums of money.

- Kathleen Mossop who, years later, saw me and my brother Jeff at a dance in the Legion Hall, and went off to fetch her friend. 'Look who I've found!' she said as she dragged (Karina Griffiths?) back to meet us. Karina had no idea who we were.

- Moses Parry, who, on the Abersoch road, held up a sign warning motorists of a speed trap up ahead. He was done for it, despite arguing that he was just trying to help the police in their efforts to get motorists to slow down and obey the law.

There were other people in the town that I don't remember at all yet were major figures. Take Victor Barma. He was a substantial and colourful figure in Pwllheli, yet, although I know the name, I remember nothing at all about him. I was aware of his sons Brian and Vicky, who were older than me, and I knew their three younger siblings Sandra, Donna and Dolwyn, who were at Penlleiniau at the same time as I was. I know that they all belonged to the Pwllheli Rock dynasty. That's the confection, not the music. Yet it's only recently, through my brother Chris and my mate Tony, that I've begun to get a sense of who Victor Barma, the father, was. Chris remembers him quite well from The Long Room, and Tony knew the whole family – they lived across the road from his parents' hotel, and both families socialised extensively.

A final category of Pwllheli townspeople are the ones of whom I had no memory at all until my mother rescued them from oblivion over the phone. A typical conversation would go something like this:

Mum: Do you remember X?

Me: No.

Mum: His mother worked in Woolworths? His father was a lifeboatman?

Me: No, sorry.

Mum: He was two years behind you at the grammar school? Went to Bangor University? Became an accountant?

Me (a memory beginning to stir): Yes, I think I do remember him. Was his sister Jeff's age, very good-looking? Did he play the violin in the County Youth Orchestra?

Mum: Yes, that's him.

Me: What about him?

Mum: He's dead.

This sort of thing happened so often when we were on the phone to Mum that my brother Chris started calling her 'Dial-a-death'.

Postscript

My mother's role as 'dial-a-death' found several echoes in the comments that followed the post:

- A relative who, when the rest of her family went on their annual six-week holiday to France, would clip all the stories of death and disaster from the local paper whilst they were away, then regale them on their return with a sort of bad-news digest – not highlights, perhaps, but lowlights. 'She couldn't fathom,' the commentator reports, deadpan, 'why they stayed away so long.'

- A Pwllheli couple, living in Ireland for many years, kept in touch by having the *Daily Post* sent to them. During a brief hiatus in the obituaries, the husband grumbled, 'I'm going to complain. There's nobody dying in Pwllheli.'

Is this obsession with death a Welsh thing? I don't think so – I've certainly come across it, for example, among Jewish writers. But then they do say that the Welsh might be the lost tribe of Israel.

Pwllheli characters

When I first went away to college in London I must have spent a lot of time rattling on to my new friends about Pwllheli – an irritating habit arising, no doubt, from extreme homesickness – because one of them said, smirking at the others, 'You seem to have a lot of real "characters" in your home town!'

I thought about it, and decided he was right. I don't know if it's a small-town thing, a Welsh thing, a small Welsh town thing or what. But since leaving home over fifty years ago, wherever I've lived there never seems to have been anywhere near the same concentration of – well – characters.

Take John Cholomondely (or it might be 'Chumley' – I've never seen his name written down). When I came back home he'd pop up (Hey, Jonathan) and recite, following me down the street and at the top of his voice, every railway station, town and village between where I then lived and Pwllheli. Or Dick Double Dutch who gave out free samples of Pwllheli Rock on the Maes and, reputedly, had a metal plate in his head. Or Bob Workhouse who walked with his head slanted to one side. Or Kelvin Kelly, who liked to lead the carnival parade. Then there was Wil Cap Coch, named presumably for his preferred headgear, and his son Ned Cap Coch, either with similar taste in head-covering, or simply named after his dad. Or was Ned the father and Wil the son? I can't remember. Or Pyrs, who ate dead matches and was always grateful for any donations. Others were almost mythical: Sam Barnes and his golden eagle. Mr May the photographer from South Beach, with his big plate camera and specs with one lens blocked off.

I knew nothing about these 'characters' – their history, background, family – apart from my own experience of them as a kid. And yet I felt that they were an integral part of the town of my childhood. London, on the other hand, when I became a student there, though exciting and stimulating (it was the '60s after all), seemed to be altogether too intimidating and anonymous. The only characters I seemed to come across slept in doorways – far more shocking then than alas it is today – or shouted at you on the Tube.

My brother Chris, a born-again adoptive Londoner, would no doubt fervently disagree.

Postscript

A couple of posts really drove home the unreliability of memory that I mentioned earlier. One post included a photo of somebody handing out Pwllheli Rock samples on the Maes. Another included a photo of Dick Double Dutch. I recognised them both, and realised that they were two different people. Yet my memory had melded them into one.

Other posts yielded a lot of additional characters, some of which I'd forgotten but could now remember, others of whom were a complete blank.

Glaring omission in my original post included Jack Benn, a major figure in Pwllheli's maritime history, Mai Papur Newydd (or was it Nel Papur Newydd? Or May Coetiwrs?) who used to deliver Sunday papers (from Bodawen Milk Bar, it was thought) in a pram, and Bernard Wakeling, who loved music, particularly Elvis.

Other suggested additions to the list I've either completely forgotten or were from before or after my time: Nee Arkle from Kings Head Street, Joe Miles, Mackerel, Taxi and Bread, Myfi Gas, Betty Thomas with her parrot, Wmffra. I don't even know if these names are accurate – is Nee Arkle correct, or a typo for Ned Arkle? Is Taxi and Bread one person or two? Was Wmffra actually Humphrey? I'm beginning to see that this makes Pwllheli sound like an alternative Llareggub, or an updated *Guys and Dolls*, but I can't help that.

Many of the names put forward in the comments were just that – names, totally shorn of context. Others came with brief details of who they were. Some even came with photographs. But all, when added to the memories of friends, family members, schoolmates, teachers and acquaintances, have contributed to the portrait of the vibrant, inclusive town that I remember Pwllheli to have been.

A final comment. It was brought home to me that this host of people who, to me, were 'characters', were in fact people, with their own backgrounds and biographies. As I said before, they were the stars in their own lives, and I was just one of a cast of thousands in theirs.

CHAPTER 8

Leaving Pwllheli

As the infant takes its first frightened tottering steps, as the fledgling quivers on the branch before launching itself into space, as the ... Well, you get the idea. Leaving home is a REALLY BIG DEAL!

Apart from quitting the womb and coming out into the light of day (and thank God I can't remember that), leaving Pwllheli after eighteen years, especially to go to one of the biggest cities in the world, has to come next in terms of trauma. Yet the process of separation was, after the first shock, surprisingly long drawn out. Contact with friends carried on, if slowly fading. Contact with family continued unabated, though after the death of my parents, usually away from Pwllheli – in Doncaster and Birmingham, in Manchester and London, in Ipswich and Yorkshire and Stoke.

He's leaving home

The period between O- and A-Level was one when you increasingly felt that you were betwixt and between – outgrowing school, but too nervous to be making your own way in the world. Or like a hermit crab, finding the old protective shell too restrictive, looking to move on and find a bigger, better one.

Tony and I left Pwllheli to go to college in the autumn of

1964. I'd have to admit that we were pretty cocky. Though, on my part at least, with an undercurrent of panic.

Tony was off to Liverpool College of Art (the same college that John Lennon went to – there he goes again, I thought, impossibly cool) to do a pre-diploma course. I was off to Swinging London, one of the great cities of the world, which was beginning to throw off its staid image as the centre of a crumbling empire and earn a reputation as the world capital of youth culture. I'd finished working in the staff canteen in Butlins, I'd packed my trunk. Tony had no doubt made his own preparations. Two boys from Pwllheli, ready to take on the world.

The reality was so, so much harder than I expected. Transitions can be frightening – ask any hermit crab. Dad came with me down to the station, carrying my suitcase (my trunk had been picked up the day before). We walked along the platform, dodging jets of steam escaping from the waiting train. I boarded, stowed my bag on the overhead string rack, leaned out of the drop-down window and awkwardly shook Dad's hand. The train crept out of the station, and the harbour slid past. I can't remember if the tide was in or out. If it was in, and the sun was shining, Pwllheli would have looked glorious – all the harder to leave. If the tide was out, with rain hammering down from an overcast sky, Pwllheli would have looked depressing, reflecting my utter dejection at leaving home. If this was growing up, it sucked.

I dashed a manly tear from my eye. In Cricieth a rabble of kids in uniform piled on, pushing and shoving, and for the next five miles created havoc. It reminded me of YRP and what I was leaving behind. The St Trinian's wannabees got off at Porthmadog, and I, together with all the other passengers on the train, heaved a sigh of relief.

I would of course be coming home during the holidays, and for the next forty years, to see friends and visit parents. But, looking back from the vantage point of my seventies, there's no doubt in my mind that this was the day that I left my childhood behind, and embarked on my adolescence.

I'm still waiting for that to end, and the period of wise maturity to begin.

It's an ill wind...

I have thought long and hard about how – or whether – to write this post. In the end I decided to go ahead, hoping that the story might be inspirational to anybody who is off to university soon, and being determined to express it with as much delicacy and sensitivity as I can muster.

So, to return to the autumn of 1964. My first few months at university in London were absolute hell. I just didn't know how to make friends. Any move by others towards friendship I interpreted as people feeling sorry for me, so I rejected them. What I considered to be my BBC received pronunciation turned out to be incomprehensible to everybody I spoke to. So lonely was I that, when I heard that Brian Clark's brother Leslie, who lived in London, was driving up to Pwllheli for the weekend, I jumped at the offer of a lift – a six-hundred-mile round trip for, in effect, a day at home. And to compound my misery, on my return to the capital my briefcase was stolen in a pub in Tottenham Court Road – all my notes so far, and several textbooks, gone. I really couldn't see me lasting out the term, never mind the three years of the course. I hated the London School of Economics, I hated England's capital city, and indeed, I hated England itself.

Then everything changed, and I owed it all to methane.

Let me explain. I was living in a hall of residence near Euston Station. At the end of two months, I knew nobody, and nobody knew me. But one night, after a solitary session in the pub with a book, I drifted back to somebody's room – the biggest, I think, in Passfield Hall, and therefore the one that tended to host continued after-hours socialising. Everybody was three sheets to the wind. During a lull in the conversation I – and there's no way to explain why I did it, and no polite way to put it – ignited an escape of methane from my nether region, using a Dunhill knock-off that I'd bought in the local market. As the rolling green and blue flame subsided there was a stunned silence followed by a disbelieving roar of approbation. All around the room people threw themselves backwards, hoisted their legs skywards, and applied matches and lighters to trousers or jeans stretched tightly over buttocks. It was the sensation of the year.

The ice was well and truly broken. From then on, people smiled at me in corridors, grinned at me over meals in the refectory, made a point of talking to me, bought me pints in the bar and in general wanted to be my friend.

From then on, I was 'the Welsh bloke who lights farts'.

How proud my parents would have been, had they known!

Postscript

The comments attached to this post ranged from the ironic ('Wonderful. Like a breath of fresh air'), through the affirmative ('Brilliant! A sure way of coaxing our young to spread their wings and fly'), to the cataclysmic (advice from the United States to 'Never light your farts with your trousers down!' Especially, it transpired, in a country which doesn't have a National Health Service).

It even led to speculation that such youthful pursuits might be harder today among us aged boomers. The comment is worth quoting in full:

> Imagine the explosion you'd cause these days even if
> you are still agile enough to twist around to have a go
> without setting fire to the tails of your shirt or your
> flapping cardigan... I can just imagine grandpas around
> the country taking off, given the increase in internal gas
> production with each passing year. It would provide
> *Fortean Times* with a rich vein of material and a whole
> spate of articles.

I had to Google *Fortean Times*. Its strapline is 'The World's Weirdest News'.

A bad week

Towards the end of my first term at university, I received an envelope which caused widespread excitement at my hall of residence. Heavily embossed with the crest of the House of Commons (the envelope, not the hall of residence), it contained an invitation to lunch from Goronwy Roberts, the Labour MP for Caernarfonshire. I don't know how I merited this invitation. I like to think it was because of my upright character, magnetic personality and general charisma. But I suspect it was more to do with the fact that his son Dafydd was in my class at YRP.

These were exciting times. Labour had just won a general election, ejecting the Tories after thirteen years, but with a wafer-thin majority. I was at that time, I'm embarrassed to admit, totally ignorant of politics. So thank God, I took my much more clued-up mate Alan Tucker with me as my plus one.

The charming Right Honourable (not yet Lord) Goronwy Roberts met us in the entrance foyer, showed us around the Palace of Westminster, introduced us to a few politicians (one was, I remember, an ex-postmaster general), then led us to the Strangers Dining Room, where we settled down to eat. My friend kept up the conversation with a series of intelligent and penetrating questions. I, sensibly, kept my mouth shut, except when stuffing it with food. But more of that later.

A waiter arrived at our table and parked a trolley next to it bearing a bewildering array of hors d'oeuvres, none of which I could have identified to save my life. So, after my MP and my mate, still chatting chummily about politics, had made their judicious choices, rather than just point and say, 'I'll have some of that', I announced breezily that I'd have a bit of everything. What I hadn't accounted for was that the handful of little buckets facing me were not alone. They were on a revolving drum, with many more hidden from view. So, inexorably, as the drum revolved, further buckets of unrecognisable food hove into view, and additional helpings of starters were added to my plate. By the time it finished, I had a mountain of food before me that put Yr Wyddfa to shame. I had to crane my neck to peer around it whilst trying to look as if I was following the conversation.

I was glad when we'd said our goodbyes and left. My ordeal was over.

Not my finest hour.

A few days later, I attended a formal dinner hosted by the academic in charge of our hall of residence. I was placed next to his wife. I'm useless at small talk, but I don't think it was her strong point either. Our total conversation:

She: 'You're Welsh?'

Me: 'Yes.'

She: 'Where are you from?'

Me: 'Pwllheli.'

She: 'Is that near Cardiff?'

Me: 'No.'

During this scintillating repartee, I was distracted by efforts to work out which cutlery to use with which course. I think I can confidently say that I got it wrong – when we arrived at the pudding, I couldn't get my very large soup spoon into the very small bowl containing my apple crumble.

Only months earlier I couldn't wait to leave Pwllheli and start my life's adventure. Now I just wanted to go home.

A Christmas story

It was just before Christmas in 1964. My father and I were driving out to a farm near Aberdaron to pick up a turkey.

Already misty when we set off from Pwllheli, it got thicker and thicker as we drove. Crawling up a hill (Mynytho? Nanhoron?), we suddenly came out of what was now a dense fog into crystal clear air. Stretching ahead and below us was a flat white sea of fog with hills jutting out like islands, all brightly lit by a full moon and a sky full of stars. Eighteen-year-old students are not noted for lyricism, but even I could see that it was magical.

We dipped into and out of the fog all the way to Aberdaron. When we got to the farm we were shown into a large kitchen. Big table, roaring fire, family members dotted around, an old lady – clearly the head of the family – wrapped in a shawl and wearing a cloth cap sitting in the corner next to the fire.

We were offered a panad (cup of tea). As we drank our tea, the conversation we'd interrupted resumed. Though pleased that the news on television was now in Welsh, the weather forecast was in English, and to a family of farmers and fishermen, most of whom were uncomfortable in English – indeed the old lady spoke only Welsh – this was quite a serious shortcoming.

A friend of the family entered and, after warming himself at the fire, took a folded copy of the local Welsh-language newspaper out of his back pocket and ('Gwrandewch' (Listen)) launched into the reading of a poem. When he'd finished, there was much head-nodding and expressions of approval.

Dad got up and went over to thank the old lady. The turkey was fetched, hands were shaken, then my father and I got into the car in the farmyard and set off back to Pwllheli.

I'd just come home after my first term at university in London. At the time, that Aberdaron farm impressed me as being typical of backward rural Wales. The old lady couldn't even speak English! What a contrast with the Swinging London I'd left just a few days earlier!

What a pillock you can be when you're eighteen.

Postscript

At the time, it was the magical drive with my dad that remained uppermost in my mind. Looking back today, it's the wonderful human warmth of the farmhouse that takes pride of place.

The quest for a turkey was just a McGuffin. However, it was memories of Christmas turkeys that provoked the majority of the comments:

- People in Pwllheli walking home on Christmas day from Bob Ellis's bakery with their cooked turkeys and geese. Their own ovens weren't big enough for the birds.

- A girl who lived on a farm being afraid of the turkeys, which were vicious. Her mother would let the dogs out to protect her when she got home from school. Eating turkey for Christmas dinner must have been a delicious form of revenge – in this one instance, best served hot.

- Other turkeys being appropriated – mainly from outlying farms, but also from John Goddard's in the bowels of the Town Hall.

In addition, the comments filled me in about the farm that Dad and I had visited in Aberdaron. It was called Tir Glyn, and the old lady with her cloth cap was a well-known character in the area.

A little research explained the complaints that the news on TV was in Welsh, but not the weather forecast. BBC Cymru had been established earlier that year, so Welsh-language TV was a novelty. But in addition to pleasure at being able to hear the news in their own language for the first time, there were widespread complaints that, in a farming and fishing community, having the weather forecast in English just wasn't good enough.

Holiday work

Being a town with a substantial tourist industry, Pwllheli offered lots of opportunities to earn money during the holidays. The biggest source of such employment was Butlins, about which I've already written. But there were others, especially when we'd left school and were at college or university.

Dick Parry's boats

In 1965, at the end of my first year at university, I had a job
to die for – working on two locally-owned speedboats taking
campers for trips around the bay off the beach at Butlins. This
was a 'concession' (i.e. the boats' owner paid Butlins for the
right to run the trips), and I therefore wasn't actually working
for the holiday camp.

Some memories:

- Owner Dick Parry tearing off to England to get
  replacements for the hundred and ten horsepower
  inboard/outboard Volvo engines for the two boats.
  Something about the bores not being true, so the cams
  were wearing down.

- Passing petrol cans back onto the boat at the end of the
  day – most empty, but some still full. Heaving an empty
  can as if it was full, so that the boss would brace to take
  the weight, then stagger backwards when the weight just
  wasn't there. Is it my imagination, or did he actually
  shoot back across the boat and plunge overboard the
  other side?

- Responding to a shout from campers during our
  lunch break ('A shark!') with a patronising laugh,
  assuming porpoises, then seeing the sinister triangular
  fin moving steadily across the mouth of the bay. We
  jumped into one of the boats and roared out towards
  the fish, expecting it to dive. No – it totally ignored
  us: a basking shark almost as long as the nineteen-foot
  boat.

- Fishing for mackerel on the way back to Baines from
  Butlins.

- Spending a whole day after a stormy night scouring a
  choppy Cardigan Bay for the gangways. In the past
  we'd left them shackled on the beach, but campers kept
  breaking them up for barbeque firewood. So we'd started

mooring them offshore. They'd broken free and sailed off towards Harlech.

- Dick's boat, following ours into Baines, suddenly veering off to the left and shooting up onto the shore. 'Steering cable snapped,' Dick called across, looking sheepish, when we went to investigate.

Lots of other memories. But what a summer job!

Postscript

Responses to this post included some from the daughters of our bosses Dick Parry, who owned the boats and drove one of them, and Billy McGill, who drove the other:

- Dick's daughter told me that jobs on the boats were highly prized among boys in the town, and that I was lucky to get one. On reflection, I think I got the job by accident – my elder brother Jeff had made enquiries, and Dick came to our house to talk to him. Jeff was out. I wasn't.

- I also heard of a dramatic incident after I left. Dick bought a brand-new boat at the Boat Show which, on its first trip out and with a full load of campers, sprang a serious leak and started to sink. Dick took off his shirt and set fire to it in order to draw attention to his plight, and another boat, seeing this unconventional distress signal, came to the rescue. Billy McGill eventually managed to salvage the boat, discovering that it had split wide open along the keel.

- I found out that Billy McGill eventually took over the business when Dick retired because of ill health. I was glad to hear that Billy, now in his late 80s, was still going strong.

Waiting on table

I've never actually worked in a restaurant, but lots in Pwllheli took on extra staff during the summer. Here's a story, set in a Pwllheli restaurant, that deserves a permanent record. The story belongs to my friend Tony Pierce, but I'm sure he won't mind my telling it. That said, I haven't asked his permission, just in case he says no. And any mistakes I make (it was, after all, over half a century ago) he can correct in due course.

Tony got a summer job waiting on tables at the Mariner Grill opposite the station. His initial training included detailed instruction on how to present the cheeseboard to customers at the end of the meal. The cheeseboard consisted of a board (of course) upon which lay the cheese selection, protected by a Perspex cover with sliding up-and-over hatch. He should, he was told, place the near end of the board on his left forearm with the other end on the table edge, then slide the cover, with a suave flourish of his right hand, up and over to allow the customers to indicate their choice of cheese.

That first night was busy, and hot. Feeling dehydrated, every time Tony visited the kitchen he helped himself to a glass of chilled white wine from a refrigerated bulk dispenser. This quenched his thirst and boosted his feeling of bonhomie but did little for his sense of balance.

The evening drew to a close. He approached his final table with the cheeseboard, and suspended it, as he'd been trained, between his left arm and the table.

That's when disaster struck.

Tony swayed backwards, and the far end of the cheeseboard and the edge of the table parted company. Dropping in an arc, the handle on the Perspex cover caught the edge of the table, sliding it open, the descending edge of the board hit the clasp of the lady's very posh handbag, springing it ajar, and the cheeses, all of them, shot into its velvet depths, one by one.

It was Tony's first and last night at the Mariner Grill.

Perhaps this is why Tony now lives in France.

Postscript

Tony contacted me from France where he lives (or maybe Spain, where he seems to spend a lot of his time) to tell me that my story was essentially accurate, but was incorrect in two respects:

1. The wine he was drinking was red, not white.
2. The event described didn't occur on his first night at the restaurant, but after several weeks of relatively blameless service. But yes, certainly on his last.

I decided that I would leave the account as I first wrote it, for the following reasons:

1. As a cooling and thirst-quenching drink, white wine is in my opinion superior to red, since it is served chilled.
2. As a climax to the story, his sacking is far more impactful if it occurs on his first night, rather than after several weeks.

I think Tony will understand this. We both studied A-Level English under Swift, who introduced us to the concept of 'poetic licence'.

Christmas postie

In the mid-1960s I worked as a relief postman in Pwllheli – students like me were taken on to help with the Christmas rush. I was allocated a handful of houses strung along the coast beyond Pwllheli Golf Club. I can only assume that it was a round that the permanent posties didn't want, and so was unloaded onto the unsuspecting newbie. But to me it was magical.

I rode a heavy red post office bike with the mail sack suspended from a frame ahead of the handlebars. I had a huge cape which covered the whole of the bike, the mail, and most of me. In bad weather, when the cape was deployed, only my head would stick out. I must have presented a rare sight – a strange beast with huge brown body and tiny head, gliding along beside the sea.

After delivering letters to the Clubhouse, I'd ride along a path through the dunes next to the tees, fairways, bunkers and greens. I'd call in at the house on the edge of the fifth green (who'd give me a cup of tea and, on my last day, a Christmas card and a pair of socks), then continue past the end of the top nine and the Boys Brigade camping ground to the farm guarded by a vicious dog chained to an upturned boat.

In between, I'd lay down my bike, sit on top of the dunes and smoke a cigarette whilst looking out across Cardigan Bay. Sometimes it was flat calm, sometimes it was wild and turbulent. Even when the rain was blowing in off the sea, I was dry inside my cape.

The job lasted ten days. But it left me, fifty-five years later, with a yardstick against which to measure peace and tranquillity. And, it has to be said, strong feelings of envy towards those in Pwllheli who live by the sea.

You lucky bastards!

The pull of Pwllheli

The influence of my home town continued unabated during my time in London.

When I got there, I met a friend from home – she was already based in the capital and offered to show me around. Good job – talk about a hick from the sticks! On my first experience of the Tube, we stood in front of one of those expanding gates, and I thought we were waiting for the lift. Then the floor dropped from under my feet – we were actually *in* the lift, and it was enormous. I tried to look nonchalant but had nearly wet myself, and couldn't suppress a yelp of surprise. My friend, fair play, kept a relatively straight face.

With Tony Pierce at Liverpool College of Art, it didn't take us long to link up. One holiday in that first year, rather than going straight back to Pwllheli from London, I arranged to go via Liverpool and meet up with Tony and my brother Jeff and his wife Ambo. We had a splendid night at the Crack, a pub, across the road to the art college, made famous by the antics of John Lennon, often kicked out for eccentric behaviour. Tony tells me I stayed with him at his aunt's house – I thought I'd slept on the floor at my brother's flat. Obviously a really good night. I decided to hitchhike home from Liverpool the next day, still no doubt under the influence of Jack Kerouac and *On the Road*. Not to mention the previous night's beer.

Since you can hardly stick your thumb out in the centre of Liverpool, I caught the underground to Birkenhead. But that didn't improve things, so I got on a bus to the main north Wales road. From there to Caernarfon took me all day – a succession of short lifts including a farmer in an Austin A35 van with several sheep in the back. I was grateful for the lift but didn't like the smell nor the amorous way the nearest sheep was looking at me.

It was dark by the time my last lift drove me into Castle Square in Caernarfon. Bugger Jack Kerouac, I thought, and caught the next bus home. I'd hitchhiked to save money but, with the underground, the buses in Birkenhead and from Caernarfon to Pwllheli, it ended up costing me twice as much as if I'd just done the whole trip by coach.

Back in Pwllheli, some time later, Tony and I were out for a pint. We'd had a good few, but were now running out of cash. We'd pooled our pitiful few coins, remnants of our term's grants, and exchanged them for a final half of mild each in the front bar of the West End Hotel. That was it, we were broke. And yet (and many will know this feeling, which should never be ignored) we had a strong conviction that the night was absolutely ripe for a session. We sobbed at the unfairness of it all. Reluctantly we prepared to accept defeat and go home. As we passed the bar, heading for the door, a miracle! A ten-bob note, just lying there on the floor. And please remember, ten shillings was enough in those far off days for a goodly number of pints! Each! God couldn't have made his feelings clearer if he'd thrust a huge fist through the clouds, one finger pointing at us, and bellowed, 'Enjoy yourselves lads!'

But we knew it was wrong. We picked that ten-bob note up and took it to the police station on Ala Road, there to be claimed, in due course, by a tearfully grateful member of the public.

Just kidding! We got absolutely hammered!

The receding tide

Since leaving Pwllheli in 1964, my links with the town have slowly faded. My father died in 1974, my mother in 2008, and several aunts in between. Friends, too. And sometimes you just lose touch. So I tried to remember the times since I left that I've linked up with people who shared my childhood.

- In my third year in London friends from Pwllheli ('the boys') all headed down to the capital to sleep on my floor. This was, I think, to mark Tony Pierce's twenty-first birthday (historical note: in those days, this was a big deal – the age at which you become an adult). So for a long weekend Garnett, Brian, Joe, Jonesy, Ginge and Tony slept in the beds of my absent flat-mates or on floors which were no less uncomfortable for being in a very posh house off Knightsbridge. Ginge (as related since by Tony) came all the way down from the Midlands (where I think he was in college) on a scooter and was frozen stiff by the time he arrived. Brian proved his sophistication by 'dropping one', then pretending to tie it to a lamppost to stop it following him. Joe insisted on exploring the sights of Soho. Beyond that, I don't remember much – alcohol, as ever, was involved and it was a long time ago.

- Our next get-together was, alas, at Ginge's funeral in Pwllheli. It was, I think, the first time that any of us had experienced the death of someone really close to us. We were the pallbearers, carrying our friend to his grave in Denio cemetery. After the formal ceremony we had our own wake, ending up in Brian's mum's house on Ffordd-y-Mela, where the unbearable fact of Ian not being there, but in the ground up on the hill in Denio, had us all in tears.

- As we continued through our twenties, general get-togethers yielded to one-to-one visits. I and my girlfriend visited Tony and his girlfriend in Swansea, where he was doing a three-year degree course in stained glass. My most vivid memory was, at dinner in his flat (we were growing up. No more nights in pubs followed by curries or kebabs) of my sneezing when I had a mouthful of spaghetti bolognese. Expelling pasta explosively through one's nose is not a good look.

- Tony and I wrote to each other often (remember those days – writing letters?). The first time, I'd lost his address so, on the envelope, described the house ('it's the white house on the left at the end of the street') together with a warning to the postman ('look out for the landlady's Yorkshire terriers. They're small but they're vicious'). The letter got through.

- Next was a visit by me and my now wife to Sandycroft to stay with Garnett and Alwena. I remember that there was a party, but little else – they were very good hosts.

- A few years later it was to Tony again, this time in Paris. Tony's flat was on the Avenue de Wagram, near the Etoile. A chic address with spectacular accommodation – gilded cage-type lift and a flat so huge that Tony's wife, children, three large dogs, mynah bird, rabbit and for all I know several elephants and a herd of white rhinos were lost in its vastness. Not to mention a full-size grand piano. One of the dogs, a lugubrious Irish Setter, would lean companionably against my leg as I sat on the sofa. From the balcony that ran around the outside of the apartment you could see the red light winking on top of the Arc de Triomphe. Tony showed us around the French capital – Louvre, Sacré-Cœur, Versailles – driving like a madman (or a Frenchman) in his Land Rover. His kids went to the same school as Charlotte Rampling's. There was no getting away from it – that word again – 'cool'!

- The last time any of the boys got together for a meal in Pwllheli wasn't so long ago – Garnett, Jonesy, Brian and me with our wives in what was once the *Liverpool Echo* office. Jonesy picked up the tab for all of us. What a star!

It seems to me that we owe it to our family, our friends, our children, to write these things down. Photographs alone can't tell the tale. The tide can leave all sorts of flotsam behind, but it can also wipe the beach clean.

Deep or what?

The child is father of the man

Digging down into childhood, it's amazing how often you can find the origins of your adult self among the memories.

- My attic room in Llŷn Street took up the depth of the house, and had sloping ceilings, huge wooden beams and a dormer window at either end. On stormy nights, I could hear the rumble of the Cardigan Bay surf to the south, the roar of the wind through the trees on the Garn to the north, the rhythmic squeaking of the sign on Mr and Mrs Parker's antique shop across the road, and, during particularly violent storms, the deep crack of maroons as the crew were summoned to the lifeboat station. All my life I've loved attic rooms with heavy beams and sloping ceilings, and I've also loved stormy nights.

- The bedroom was at the top of a tall terraced house close to the centre of Pwllheli – close enough for me to be sent to post letters at the postbox at the bottom of Salem

Terrace, collect provisions (on the slate) at Williams 80, get paraffin from West End Stores in Gaol Street, or fish and chips from Penlan Street. Hence my love of Victorian and Edwardian houses, and of living close to the centre of market towns.

- Pwllheli itself has been the model for the places I've chosen to settle in. Not in size – Pwllheli has always had a population of around four thousand, and the towns I've lived in have been twenty to thirty times as big. But, being the capital of Llŷn, Pwllheli, with its two cinemas, range of shops, cafés and pubs, weekly market in the Maes and animal mart, railway and bus station, beautiful beaches and massive harbour, two primary and two secondary schools, huge holiday camp, fire brigade and lifeboat station, had always punched well above its weight. I realised this when, in the first English town I fetched up in – Ipswich – the facilities seemed of a similar order, and the feel of the place seemed so familiar. On my first night there, I went to the cinema and, at around ten o'clock, people started leaving to catch the last bus out to the surrounding villages. Just like Pwllheli.

- Finally, in this consideration of roots, there was YRP. My choice of subjects, my profession and even my approach to life were all based on three of my teachers – Swift and Harry who taught English, and Brasso who taught history. With all due respect to the rest of the YRP staff, these were the three people that I wanted to be like. So I did arts, not sciences, at A-Level, despite having, at O-Level, won the prizes for biology and maths, I read history at university, I became a teacher, and I based my whole approach to my job (keep a sense of humour, treat pupils like adults, treat management with suspicion) on the way they seemed to approach theirs.

- As Wordsworth said, passed on by Swift during A-Level English, 'The child is father of the man'.

Pwllheli – even when you've left, you haven't!

I left Pwllheli for college fifty-six years ago. Yet, even today, if I'm reading a newspaper, say, or leafing through a magazine, and the word 'Pwllheli' is part of the text, it leaps off the page. It's not just a word, it's a world – it's houses spread around a huge harbour on the Irish Sea hunkered down beneath the Garn, it's a school on a hill thronged with kids in bottle green uniform, it's long beaches and Marram grass, it's dour chapels and churches and pubs that smelled of beer and tobacco smoke, it's a town thronged with farmers on market days, it's the setting for a thousand childhood adventures and rites of passage, all set among hills and farmland next to the sea. Above all it is people – family and friends mainly, but also a huge cast of teachers and doctors and dentists and shopkeepers and ministers and councillors and fishermen and bus drivers and policemen and ... all the rest. And characters. And a hundred anecdotes. And the Welsh language.

The tentacles of the town never quite relinquish their grip. You stay tied to it – via family, via friends. To start with, when you visit, it's just you, then you and your wife, then you and your family, your children and grandchildren. But Pwllheli is always there, in the background.

After I retired, and particularly after my mother's death removed any need for me to visit Pwllheli at all, I became aware that my memories of childhood were fading away. If you live where you were brought up, you're laying down new memories all the time which integrate with, and strengthen, the memories of long ago. For exiles like myself, this doesn't happen.

Then I came across the Facebook group *Ysgolion Pwllheli & District Schools*. Reading posts, looking at photos and video clips, putting my own posts up, reading the comments, the memories have flooded back. I feel I've snatched my childhood back from the brink of oblivion.

It's true. I thought I'd left, but I haven't. And I'm glad.

Postscript

It was clear from the responses to this post that:

- A lot of Pwllheli exiles feel as I do about the town, that it is ever-present, even unconsciously, at the back of your mind.

- Like many Facebook posts, it also gave me a window into the experiences of others growing up in Pwllheli. Chapel-going, for example. During the eighteen years of my life in Pwllheli, the only time I ever set foot in a chapel was a one-off visit for a school speech day. I had no idea, for example, that Baptists still went in for total immersion. A comment described the 'paddling pool normally hidden under the carpet of the "sêt fawr" (deacons' pew)' in which the ceremony was performed. Who could fail to be moved by the account of this young girl waiting her turn, wearing a borrowed dress, and with a 'powdery swirl leaking out of my newly-whitened plimsolls'. She was glad of her parents' pride and the sense of community among chapelgoers, whilst also being aware of her own scepticism. The sense of the passage of time was palpable in the jump from that remembered rite of passage to the chapel as it is today – a furniture and bric-a-brac showroom.

- Other comments updated me, not always with approval, on changes that have happened since I left Pwllheli. The 'huge harbour' is no longer huge, but has been partly filled in to create a 'dog lavatory'. The prom has been altered in ways that not everybody likes. I think I shall revisit soon, with some trepidation.

Children and grandchildren

Of course, I shouldn't restrict myself to my own recollections of Pwllheli. One of the great pleasures of my life since leaving has been seeing my children, and then their children, enjoying the Llŷn Peninsula in some of the ways that I once did.

My son, when he was a baby, liked playing on the beach in Pwllheli, and in particular he loved eating sand and stones. Carrying him on my shoulders, I'd wondered why he seemed to be getting heavier as the day wore on. We didn't realise that he was doing it until we changed his nappy.

Getting older, there were two things that my kids enjoyed above all others on our visits to Pwllheli, and they were related:

- Collecting money. When we arrived, they extracted tribute from my parents. Then we did the rounds – to Auntie Annie May in Church Street and Auntie Eva in Talcymerau Mawr. I sometimes felt like a mafia foot soldier collecting protection money. Then there were my friends, friends of my parents, shopkeepers and general passers-by encountered in the street, all good for the odd two-bob or half a crown, and (a nice little earner this) the ladies who, with my mother, changed the flowers at St Peter's church. This was my daughter Catherine's particular patch, since she and Mum were thick as thieves – Mum had given birth only to boys, so she really welcomed her two granddaughters (one each from me and my brother). I realised this when, looking at a picture of me as a toddler, dressed in a frilly onesie (I think they were called 'siren suits'), Jeff once said, 'You can tell that Mum wanted a girl.' Older brothers can be so cruel.

- Spending the money. There were few times in their lives when they had so much of it, and they were released into town on their own, where they could spend it without any interference from us parents – in Woolworths,

Peacocks, Smiths, Caxtons and, on Wednesdays, on the Maes. They loved, too, the boat-swings and rides and penny arcade machines in Studt's funfair. On one visit my son toddled off without telling us to have his picture taken in the photograph booth. He didn't realise that you had to adjust the seat to allow for different heights. When his strip of pictures came out, all four showed the white background and, at the very bottom of the frame, a small tuft of his hair. We tried not to laugh – he was very down-in-the-mouth ('cêg gam' I think it is in Welsh). That was two shillings of his protection money down the drain.

We had to prepare for our trips to north Wales carefully. At one point when he was very little, our son Daniel had fallen into the habit, every time he was overtaken by flatulence, of shouting, 'I farted', and laughing hysterically. We became worried about this as our next visit to Pwllheli approached – my Auntie Eva, as she got older, had become more and more prim, even prudish. So we spent weeks training him to say 'wind' instead of fart. Sure enough, on our next visit to Auntie Eva's flat, Dan let rip. We held our breath, and not just for the obvious reason. 'I did a wind,' he announced. We breathed out, and smiled at each other in relief. 'It's not a fart,' he continued cheerfully, 'it's a wind.'

Our holidays in Pwllheli were mainly remembered for long days on the beach, swimming, building sandcastles and eating ice cream. Apart from South Beach and West End, favourites were Cricieth and Llanbedrog. Who could ask for more – lovely sands within easy reach of food, drink and ice cream? And toilets.

Into my children's teens, the drive from the Potteries became part of the holiday, with, in Llangollen, picnics by the river and visits to the second-hand bookshop; then, in Porthmadog, the vinyl Aladdin's cave that was Cob Records. Pwllheli was a saviour, too, when we were at our wits end trying to keep

French exchange students occupied. Each of our kids in turn had teenagers over from Limoges, who will, I hope, have fond memories of approaching sheep in fields, of galloping along the shore at Llanbedrog on hired horses, or of having a crack at underage driving on Black Rock Sands.

There was something of a lull as the children grew up and flew the nest. Then, after the turn of the millennium, Llŷn began to come into its own again:

- Newly retired, I started writing articles for caravan magazines – you've got to do something with your time! In particular, I wrote three pieces about the Llŷn Peninsula. I went all over, mostly places I knew well but some that I didn't, taking photos and talking to people involved in tourism. I came to realise even more what a brilliant place Llŷn is for families with kids.

- Grandchildren started to arrive. Here we go again, I thought. Time to introduce the next generation to my home town and also, in Llanystymdwy to the rabbit farm, in Cricieth to the beach, the castle and Cadwaladers' ice cream, in Porthmadog to the Ffestiniog Railway, in Caernarfon to the castle, and, on the way to Caernarfon, to Glasfryn Parc.

We were now too big a family to impose ourselves on my elderly mother, so we camped – once in Abererch and another time in Llanbedrog (on a site, it turned out, run by my classmate Garfield Kif's sister and her husband). My grandson, two years old, tiny, and with hair so fine and blond that he looked bald, had the diners at the Glyn-y-Weddw in stitches by honking the bulb of his toy horn, using the resulting vacuum to stick it onto his forehead, then laughing fit to burst!

After Mum's death, visits to Pwllheli became few and far between. In 2014, my daughter chose to celebrate her fortieth birthday in north Wales (staying in yurts just outside Y Ffôr), and my wife and I were invited along. Our last visit, in 2018, was to mark the occasion of our golden wedding. We splashed out on a house for the whole family in Portmeirion – a previous visit for Emyr Wyn Jones's sixtieth birthday made us realise that this was possible. It was great – that superior feeling when the day visitors had to leave, the kids swimming in the little kidney-shaped pool, day trips to Porthmadog, Cricieth, Pwllheli and Llanbedrog, the final-night meal at the hotel.

On this visit I took my youngest grandchild Arianwen to Llys Pedr in Llŷn Street, and, standing outside the house and indicating points of interest like a tour guide, I told her that I'd been born in the front bedroom on the middle floor, that my room as I grew up had been the one above it on the top floor, that coal had been delivered by sliding the big slate step at the front and sending it down the chute into the cellar, and that the drainage hole in the wall of the little front garden was where I would hide my taflar ('catapult', I explained) before entering the house.

'Any questions?' I asked finally.

She looked relieved to get a word in.

'When can we go to the beach?'

Sometimes the young have no sense of history.

Late visits to Pwllheli

During the last few years of my mother's life, I often visited Pwllheli on my own, since I was retired but my wife was still working. It fell to me as the head of the family, to step up to the plate – my oldest brother had died and my youngest was still working fulltime in London. I did the trip from the Potteries every six to eight weeks, to make sure she was OK and reassure her that she hadn't been forgotten. She used to say that, when she died, most people hearing about it, if they remembered her at all, would say with surprise that they thought she'd died a long time ago.

I enjoyed these visits. I'd do various tasks on her behalf – phone the council, contact the doctor, speak to 'Cymorth Llaw', that sort of thing. Then we'd sit and chat in the back room at Penlleiniau, and though she was often quite grouchy when dealing with the present, she could be really articulate and interesting, with almost total recall, when talking about the distant past.

All this left me plenty of time to roam:

- I strolled through town and out to Talcymerau. My Auntie Eva had lived in a ground-floor flat in the big house ('Talcymerau Mawr'), and I vaguely remembered a path that ran from there to the end of Ala Road. Sure enough, there it was, and much shorter than I remembered. It was a sunny spring day, full of birdsong. I was suddenly startled by a loud clang. The path ran next to the green of what was, when I played golf, the eleventh hole of Pwllheli Golf Club. Since the fairway ran up to, then down from, a hill, the green wasn't visible from the tee, so a large bell had been hung on a post which golfers were instructed to ring when they'd finished putting. I peered through the gorse, and a golfer (in plus-fours! Honestly!) tipped his hat to me as he followed his partners to the next tee. Further along the path, as I approached the flat stone bridge with the river sliding past between the reeds and the sun beating down, the air was alive with electric blue dragonflies. There are worse places to have grown up, I thought.

- I climbed up Llŷn Street, past the house I was brought up in, intending to go around the Garn. But just before the brow of the hill, I turned off, to check out Panorama. This was, as I recalled, a steep path, some of it stepped, down to Ala Road. There might once have been views – there was a loop of the path with a bench from which to enjoy them – but even when I was a kid there were far too many trees and far too much undergrowth for you to be able to see anything. I walked down the main path, past a steep field where my brother Jeff and his mates (John Prys and Jeff Wyn, I think) had tried to get on a horse which was tethered there. The horse, with an air of bored indifference, had lazily raised one hind leg and kicked out, sending Jeff cartwheeling down the slope. He couldn't have been hurt – he was in fits. As I walked out onto Ala Road, I remembered the grove of bamboo that grew in the corner of the vicarage garden – we once knocked and got permission from Canon Evans's wife to cut some to make bows and arrows.

- I struggled along the dunes to Gimblet Rock in a howling gale. Waves crashed onto the shore and, when they hit the rock, hurled themselves into the air. As I walked, the thunder of the surf as the waves arrived alternated with the roar of the cascading shingle as they withdrew. The sea in all directions was a wilderness of white horses. When I got to the rock a childhood memory flickered out of nowhere. On such days we'd pit our wits against the sea. We'd wait on the beach until the water had withdrawn between waves, then dash for the rock face, scrambling up it before the next wave arrived. Success entitled you to stand at the top of the rock face, jeering as the water failed to reach you. If you mistimed your run by even a split second, the next wave would engulf you, leaving you drenched and gasping for air. We called the game, 'Defying the waves of Allah.' Where on earth that came from I've no idea!

One of the problems with knowing a place over more than seventy years is that memories coagulate. I couldn't swear that the above three accounts were of individual visits in the early years of the twenty-first century, or whether they were an amalgam of many adult visits at that time intertwined with earlier childhood memories. So – if the Vicarage bamboos were uprooted in 1982 or the bell on the eleventh green disappeared before the turn of the century – that's my excuse.

My final anecdote is, though, specific to one visit, in 2003, five years before Mum died. She was in her late eighties. After supper I decided to go to the Mitre for a pint.

'I'm off for a drink,' I said.

'You'll be back by nine o'clock,' she snapped.

I was a teenager again. I couldn't keep the whine out of my voice.

'But I'm fifty-seven!'

Nostalgia for good or ill

It has occurred to me, reading back over my posts about my Pwllheli childhood, that I could be accused of romanticising it. But isn't that the essence of nostalgia – that you remember the good stuff with affection, and the bad stuff seems, over time, to have just faded away?

Yes, of course, there was bad stuff. Deaths, for example, and not the deaths of elderly relatives with which we're all familiar, but deaths that cut off lives before they'd really got started and affected us deeply.

- Ginge's death I've already written about. It affected everybody who knew him. How could someone with such an appetite for life die so young? Someone survive blowing several fingers off with a bomb, yet be killed by (I think) an innocuous cut sustained in a motorcycle accident at 5mph?

- Garfield Kif, in my class and very bright. The son of a doctor in Llanaelhaearn, he sat his A-Levels, full of life and with university place assured, and was dead of meningitis before his (excellent) results came out.

- Benny Roberts, younger brother of Robert, John, Wil and Katrin Ellen, killed instantly in a motorcycle accident.

- A boy (Peter Blake's brother) who got his foot trapped at the entrance to the harbour and was drowned by the incoming tide before he could be rescued.

I'm sure everybody remembers deaths that have haunted

them throughout their lives. Deaths that shook, or destroyed, their faith in God.

And it wasn't just deaths. Growing up is a painful process of making mistakes and learning by trial and error. In friendships. In relationships with parents, with siblings, with the opposite sex. There are bound to be bad memories as well as good. Together they made us the people we are. As such, they've earned their place in our picture of the past. Nostalgia doesn't have to be rose-tinted. It can be realistic, warts and all.

The name *and* the game

You can take the boy out of Wales, as they say, but you can't take Wales out of the boy:

- Yesterday, searching for a way of describing somebody, a word popped into my head and immediately blurted out of my mouth. 'Crinc'! Is this name for 'an idiot', a word local to north Wales, or even Pwllheli? I've certainly not heard it since I moved to England.

- Talking to my daughter's primary school class about life when I was a child ('in the olden days'), I explained the rules of 'Fish-in-the-net' as operated on Penlleiniau's playground. One kid was 'it', the rest were fish. When 'it' tagged another kid, they became a 'net' of two. This net caught more and more fish, with the net getting longer and the number of fish getting smaller. Finally, it was all net, no fish. Not a bad metaphor for the depletion of our seas, come to think of it! The next day, my daughter told me, there was a full-blooded game of 'fish-in-the-net' going on in her playground – in Stoke-on-Trent!

Poetry and art

I caught myself wondering the other day why my childhood memories of Llŷn are so vivid, after all this time. Obviously frequent visits, up to my mother's death in 2008, had a lot to do with it. But I've since visited only twice in thirteen years, yet my emotional connection to the area continues unabated, even grows. Perhaps absence really does make the heart grow fonder.

Thinking back over my time living in England, though, made me realise that, unlikely though it may seem, the poetry and art of Llŷn has played a part in keeping me, emotionally at least, in touch with my roots. Specifically, one poet and one painter.

The poet was (and is) Christine Evans. I came across her first collection, *Looking Inland*, in 1984, the year after it was published. On the map on the cover, Pwllheli crept into the right-hand margin. I loved the book. I still think that first collection is my favourite – poems about farming and fishing on Llŷn, of household routines and village life, of teaching in Pwllheli, of living for part of each year on Bardsey. There's even a lovely poem about how she fits writing in between her chores as teacher, housewife, farmer.

Christine Evans joined the staff of YRP after I left, and so she never taught me. But she certainly taught my brother Chris at Glan-y-Môr. She is evidently hugely well-reckoned in Wales. The seven books of her poetry that I own (I think that may be her total published output) paint a word-picture of Llŷn that takes my breath away. Yes, yes, I'm sure if she'd taught me English, she would have castigated me for using such a cliché, but I can't think of a better way of putting it.

The painter is Simon van de Put. I don't know anything about art, as the saying goes, but I know what I like. His pictures made me look with fresh eyes at my home town, at the view from Salem Terrace and the top of Llŷn Street, at kissing-gates, at old farm implements with grass growing through them, at views of Abersoch and Llanbedrog and Aberdaron, at the bays and headlands of the peninsula.

I have two prints of Simon van de Put's paintings on my walls. I couldn't afford originals. But my younger brother has a commissioned original, and it's a beaut. After our father died, our mother commissioned Simon to do a picture of Penlleiniau School, where Dad had been headteacher for forty years. It captures the essence of the building and evokes a flood of memories of my childhood. What more could you ask of an artist?

Three further observations:

- My copy of Christine Evans's *Island of Dark Horses* includes handwritten thanks to the provider of the cover photograph – Peter Hope Jones, giant of British ornithology, frequent visitor to Bardsey and friend of R.S. Thomas. How his copy of the book ended up on my shelf I've no idea – it can't have been sold on the dispersal of his estate, since I bought it ages ago, and he died only last year. I am, however, delighted to own a book with such distinguished provenance.

- Simon van de Put's daughter announced on Facebook that her dad was selling a lot of his paintings. He is presumably, as so many of us are at our age, looking to downsize. I later contacted him to investigate the possibility of using one or two of his pictures as illustrations for this book, and to ask what fee this might involve. He immediately granted unconditional permission, said he would charge no fee, and wished me luck.

- The other thing which has kept me in touch with Pwllheli and Llŷn is, of course, and it goes without saying, membership of the *Ysgolion Pwllheli & District Schools* Facebook group, to which I've belonged since 2013.

Postscript

- A lot of the comments involved high praise for Christine Evans as a teacher. Indeed, one of these glowing endorsements came from beyond the grave – Maldwyn, a popular YRP teacher now presumably deceased, provided a glowing testimonial via his daughter.

- Several ex-pupils who remember Christine Evans fondly as a teacher had no idea that she was, and is, one of Wales's finest poets, and immediately vowed to buy copies of her books.

- One of the comments came from an ex-pupil who has lived in Tasmania for over forty years. All that time, and the 'hiraeth' persists!

- Another, who still lives in Pwllheli, sometimes chats with Christine Evans in the veg aisle of Lidl. Shades of the 'Lake Isle of Innisfree'!

- There were comments by, and about, Christine Evans's successor at Glan-y-Môr school, who is a member of the group. She got rave reviews, with one, in Welsh, saying that her enthusiasm was contagious (heintus). The 'translate' button rendered this as 'leprous'!

- It was suggested that Christine Evans's son runs a ferry from Aberdaron to Bardsey Island. If Covid allows a visit to Pwllheli, I hope to check this out.

CHAPTER 9

Wales and the Welsh

IT WASN'T UNTIL I joined the *Ysgolion Pwllheli & District Schools* Facebook group that I started posting memories of growing up in Pwllheli. Reading the resulting comments, I began to address my feelings about Wales and being Welsh. How could it take over half a century to think about something so fundamental?

On Welsh and being Welsh

During my childhood and teens I and my mates spoke English amongst ourselves, even though some of us were fluent in Welsh. I wasn't – my Welsh was poor, I suppose because we spoke English at home. Mum spoke no Welsh. Dad was bilingual and spoke Welsh at home only to *his* mother, who lived with us. And it was a peculiar version of the language – south Walian Welsh.

At school Welsh was compulsory to O-Level, but there were three sub-levels: 03 was, if I remember rightly, for non-Welsh speakers, often English kids who'd recently moved into the area; 01 ('hard Welsh') was for native speakers, and consisted of separate language and literature papers; 02 was somewhere in between, aimed at kids who had one Welsh and one English-speaking parent. I took 02. My vocabulary was fair, but 'treigliadau' (mutations) and verb conjugation would tie me up in knots. And there were other subtleties that passed me by – I remember my classmates suppressing giggles when I addressed Welsh teacher Mair in the second person singular, and therefore over-familiar 'ti' rather than in the more formal, and more appropriate, second person plural 'chi'.

Today I can usually follow Facebook posts in Welsh – they're written as people talk, though I often need to use my online Welsh dictionary for particular words. When I listen to the TV or radio news in Welsh, however, or to a Welsh football commentary, they might as well be speaking Klingon.

As for being Welsh we didn't seem to think much about it. I suppose we had nothing else to compare it with. We certainly felt Welsh when watching international rugby, but otherwise there was even a definite anti-Welsh feeling abroad in Pwllheli, a feeling that being Welsh was something to be ashamed of. As I got older, though, I started becoming aware of Welsh nationalism. A lad called Lodge at school gave me a pamphlet laying out the case for independence which I found persuasive. I particularly remember a breakdown of how much was extracted in taxes from Wales, and how little benefit Wales got in return. I was aware, too, of the Tryweryn controversy – one of the bombers was the guy I'd spent my youth paying for drinks in his Expresso Coffee Bar. It was a penny cheaper if you ordered in Welsh, and my Welsh was at least up to that.

After leaving Pwllheli for London, I became far more conscious of my nationality. For a start, as I mentioned earlier, my fondly imagined Received Pronunciation turned out to be incomprehensible to the English ear.

In later life, when I had to phone home and talk to somebody I didn't know – a campsite, for example, or 'Cymorth Llaw' (home help) on behalf of my elderly mother, they would hear my accent and immediately switch to Welsh. I would explain, in English, that my Welsh wasn't good enough to deal with the matter at hand. They would courteously switch back to

English, but with a distinct edge of disappointment, a subtle form of language-shaming. And they were right – I did feel ashamed.

My attempts to put matters right have, I'm afraid, been less than impressive. I drove to Nant Gwrtheyrn to suss out possible courses but took it no further. I went into Llên Llŷn on the Maes to ask for *Teach Yourself Welsh*. I discovered that the owner was somebody who'd been in my class at school – Mac – and he advised me instead to buy a Welsh novel and a dictionary, then work my way through. I tried, but to no avail. I watched *Pobol y Cwm* on TV but found the mixture of north and south Welsh totally confusing. I've had to accept defeat – if I couldn't become fluent in the eighteen years I lived full-time in Pwllheli, one of the most Welsh-speaking towns in Wales, then there'd be little chance, at seventy-five, that I'm suddenly going to 'get it'.

I'm just not a linguist. But still very proud to be Welsh.

Postscript

Comment about the Welsh language was prolonged and detailed. I was startled at the amount of common ground the discussion revealed:

- Many of us shared the experience of the split between English and Welsh, usually the result of having one parent who spoke Welsh and one who didn't. As one person put it, 'Welsh blood, English heart.'

- The chasm between north and south Welsh also came up a lot. A Swansea landlady and her Pwllheli student tenant trying, and failing, to understand each other, and the unholy mixture of north and south Welsh on *Pobol y Cwm* that I've already mentioned that led to a claim that the programme had at one point north Welsh subtitles. Surely not!

- One person who left north Wales at a relatively young age speculated that, when she returns, her Welsh must sound, to those who never left, like a blast from some sort of Victorian past.

- Accents also came up, and the fact that all it takes for our accents to revert to that of our childhood is a conversation on the phone with somebody from north Wales.

- My fear of getting into a prolonged conversation in Welsh was also shared by many. You may be fluent in the commonplace phrases of idle chat, but it doesn't mean that you can handle a lengthy and nuanced political debate or philosophical discussion. Or even an explanation of how to get to the toilet.

I thank the Lord I'm Welsh

Being Welsh is like belonging to a secret society. Instead of a special handshake, we recognise each other by our accents. We can spot a fellow Welshman or Welshwoman within the first few words of a conversation. Then 'Where are you from?' leads inevitably to the tracking down of connections through friends, families, acquaintances. Never mind the 'six degrees of separation' – we'd be disappointed if it took us more than three.

Here are a few of the members of the society who I've come across during my life:

At university in London:

Tudor Thomas: From Cardigan. He was an excellent rugby player who, whilst easily good enough for the college first team, preferred to play in the thirds. His explanation? 'The first team takes it too seriously.' A big, powerfully-built full back and goal-kicker, he surprised us by being able to get tiddly on the smell of a cork.

In schools I've taught at:

Dick Hannaford: A south Walian woodwork teacher, he helped me build a small bookcase which my grandson, fifty years later, still uses, tried unsuccessfully to teach me the rudiments of sailing on the River Orwell, and gave me a memorable example of how to deal with those higher up the management pecking-order than yourself. After muted shouting in the marking area, he walked out into the staffroom, turned back to his red-faced head of department who was following him out, and snapped, 'And you can put that where the monkey puts his nuts.'

Mike Evans: From Aberporth. He involved me in playing rugby for an Ipswich works team (Ransoms, Simms and Jeffreys, since you ask). He was responsible, after a weekend away with our wives, and courtesy of a full bottle of whisky, for my first ever 'sickie'. When my son was born, prematurely, on a visit to see him and his wife after they'd move to Welwyn Garden City, we indulged in the traditional 'wetting of the baby's head with Southern Comfort'. I've never drunk it since.

Dai Williams: From the Valleys, head of geography. He was a fervent socialist who taught me how to manage local elections. His son nurtured an imaginary pride of lions under the kitchen sink until his parents, thinking the obsession had gone on long enough, took him to a zoo. He was instantly cured – he'd had no idea that lions were so big!

Liz Thomas: A south Walian. When I first met her, she immediately recognised me from my accent as a 'Gog' (a rather contemptuous south Walian term for us north Walians which I'd never heard before, arising from the Welsh word for north – 'Gogledd').

Emyr Wyn Jones: With the final member of my Welsh secret society – the Taffia, if you will – I've cheated. He was actually a blast from the past rather than someone I recognised from his accent. When I lived in South Yorkshire I suffered from recurring nosebleeds and was eventually hospitalised at Doncaster Royal Infirmary. As I waited in A&E, I saw a hospital staff diagram, with names and mugshots. Right at the top of the pyramid was the Medical Director, a Dr Emyr Wyn Jones. A Welshman, I thought, and obviously doing very well for himself – it was a huge hospital. I took a closer look at the picture. 'Well blow me,' I thought, 'what are the chances.' It was Emyr, younger brother of Myron, older brother of Iorwen, who'd lived next-door-but-one to us in Llŷn Street throughout my childhood. He told the nurses to, 'Treat Mr Simon well – he's a friend of mine'. Exactly right – we members of secret societies should look out for each other. Much later in life I attended his sixtieth birthday celebration in Portmeirion, and his mother Buddug, whose funeral I attended at Penmount, became, for me, a model of how to deal with old age gracefully and with humour.

These are the people I got to know well. There were hundreds of others, in schools, pubs, libraries, record offices, campsites, every aspect of my life. I could even come across fellow-members of this international Cymdeithas Gymraeg whilst renewing my car insurance or booking a hotel over the phone. Superficial maybe, but in each case a couple of minutes conversation would set my emotional ties to Wales vibrating, fan the embers of a 'hiraeth' (longing) whose presence I hadn't suspected, and even thicken my accent so that I sounded as if I'd just come in from milking the cows.

Split personality

I've come to realise since leaving Wales that, when I lived there (1946–68), the north and the south were two different countries, with different accents when speaking English and different dialects when speaking Welsh. One a land of poetry the other of song, one rural the other industrial, one fond of football the other of rugby. And there seemed little, apart from common nationhood, to bind them together – certainly not, in my experience, a decent transport system. More of that later.

Yet I've also come to realise that, in this divided nation, I was fortunate to have a foot in both camps. Born and brought up in Pwllheli, my parents were from Ferndale, a pit village in the Rhondda. So my childhood was thronged with not only south Walian parents, but also grandparents and uncles and aunts and cousins, and punctuated by frequent, and much looked-forward-to, trips down South.

The transport connections between north and south Wales were, as I've said, dire. For a long time we didn't have a car, so when, as a small child, I went to south Wales with my mother, we travelled by train. It took sixteen hours, involved seven changes, and included a stretch on the narrow-gauge Talyllyn Railway. Even then, the rail journey didn't get us all the way – my Uncle Owen would meet us in Merthyr Tydfil and drive us the last fourteen miles over the mountain to Ferndale.

When we finally did have a car, the trip, with no motorways or dual carriageways, and with a series of busy market towns to be negotiated, took a full day, even though it was less than a hundred and sixty miles.

I've already written at length about Pwllheli as a great place in which to grow up. What really made my visits to Ferndale special was the total contrast between my parents' home-town and my own. The ribbons of terraced houses following the contours of the bare mountain. The streets joining them so steep that the pavements were flights of steps. The winding gear of the pits – over fifty in that short valley. The massive Workmen's Hall, built by the miners themselves, providing the village with a library, cinema, lecture rooms and snooker hall.

In no particular order, I remember the racket as sheep that had wandered in off the mountain rummaged in dustbins in the lane at the back of my grandparents' house, the sound of the hooter at change of shifts, the tramp of the miners going down to the pit in the valley bottom in the early morning mist (or did I lift this from *How Green was my Valley*? I'm not sure). Above all, I remember family. Is there any better feeling in the world for a kid than being abandoned by your mother (who immediately reverted to her own childhood when she entered her parents' house) to be spoilt and indulged by grandparents and uncles and aunts that you didn't see very often? In a house with a model of a galleon under full sail in a glass case above the kitchen door? That had crates of pop delivered like milk from a float, and stored in the twll-dan-grisiau (cupboard-under-the-stairs)? Where you could make toast in front of the kitchen fire using a brass toasting fork? Where you had to use an outside loo, and wipe yourself on newspaper cut into squares, which left ink all over your bum? (Hang on. This last wasn't so wonderful. It was really cold in winter, and there were spiders and cobwebs!)

As a teenager things were even better. I was free to roam, to go to the pictures on my own, to sit in Fessies café, smoke, drink coffee, put records on the juke box and, agreeing with Elvis, feel ineffably sad that I was in love with the girl of my best friend, even though I didn't have a best friend, he didn't have a girl, and I wasn't in love with her anyway. To go down the hill to Auntie Ann's corner shop, where she'd slip me a couple of packets of Senior Service off the shelf then follow me into the back room where I could have a smoke and a natter like a grown-up. Or, when my older brother was there, to slope off to play snooker at the Workmen's Hall, sure that we'd hoodwinked everybody with our claim that we were going for a walk up the mountain, only for Dad to say as we left the kitchen, 'Make sure you don't rip the cloth'? Or go to Cardiff to St Fagans folk museum or to watch top-class rugby? Or visit the Weston-super-Mare branch of the family in Uncle Owen's car by crossing the Severn Estuary on a tiny car ferry that looked like a tub?

I always envied those of my friends whose families had lived in Pwllheli for generations. They seemed to have uncles and aunts and cousins everywhere, and grandparents who they saw all the time, and who had all the time in the world for them. But now, looking back, I appreciate that living in the north but with an extended family in the South had its own advantages. Two totally different towns in which to grow up, separated by some of the most beautiful countryside in Western Europe.

I felt like two different people, in Pwllheli and Ferndale. A split personality.

A bit like Wales, really.

Postscript

I was surprised at how many others had one foot in Llŷn and the other in Dolgellau, Porthcawl, Llanelli or Pontycymer. Comments included:

- A non-Welsh-speaking lad, staying with family in north Wales, who genuinely thought that another lad speaking Welsh was talking English, but with a speech impediment.

- Mention of outdoor loos, with their resident spiders, provoked many heartfelt and horror-stricken memories of these black holes. The outdoor toilets at Ysgol Trefor were colonised by the big kids playing something called 'tic petis'. This alas made the toilets a no-go area for more nervous little kids. I have my own memories of bursting to go to the toilet in Penlleiniau when I was in the infants but being too afraid of the older kids making fun.

- An anecdote which summed up the north/south divide will be for ever stuck in my mind. 'Gogs,' a south Walian said to a visitor from Pwllheli, 'are like piles. When they come down and then go back up, that's fine. But when they come down and stay down, that's when they become a pain in the arse.'

A common English misconception

Although born and brought up in a Welsh-speaking part of Wales, I've lived in England for over fifty years. During that time, there's a certain conversational meme that has been repeated time and time again, one that I'm sure other expats have also experienced.

When you tell a new English acquaintance that you're from Wales, the conversation goes something like this:

'Whereabouts in Wales?'

'Pwllheli.'

If they're working class, this might lead to 'I spent several years on holiday/working at Butlins. Great times.' If they're middle class it's more likely to be 'We had wonderful holidays on the Llŷn [with a fair attempt at the pronunciation] when I was a child – we used to rent a cottage every year in Abersoch. For the sailing, you know.'

You wait politely for what you know is coming.

'I love Wales, and the people are wonderful. But I have to say that one thing was a bit off. When we first walked into pubs, everybody would be speaking English then, as soon as they realised we were English, they'd switch to Welsh.'

All I can do is roll my eyes. I cannot count the number of times I've heard this. And it has come from otherwise sensible, empathetic, admirable people. Several of my friends are English. Indeed, after fifty years away from the Principality, *most* of my friends are English. And even they have repeated this tired old chestnut.

I've given a lot of thought as to why this should be. My conclusion is as follows:

Welsh is one of the oldest languages in Europe. In recent times, as new words are added every year to the English lingua franca, spoken Welsh becomes more and more dotted with Anglo-American imports. As I understand it, attempts have been made to come up with uniquely Welsh translations, but these rarely catch on. So, for example, though there is a Welsh word (teledu) for television, in my experience most Welsh speakers simply use the English word, with a strong Welsh accent, and with the emphasis on the third rather than the first syllable.

An interesting digression. My friend Joe told me that he'd heard on good authority that there was a special unit at Aberystwyth University charged with creating Welsh substitutes for common English and American imports. He went further, and claimed that sometimes, when a member of the group came up with a particular corker, they would sit around the table in hysterics, holding their sides and with tears rolling down their cheeks.

If such a unit ever did exist, it shared with countries all over the world an admirable but doomed attempt to keep the languages pure. The French, with their war against Franglais, would, I'm sure, be particularly sympathetic.

To get back to the point. I believe that, when English visitors enter a Welsh-speaking pub, what happens is that they listen to the hum of general conversation as they make their way to their table, recognise a few English words and assume that everybody is speaking English. Then, when they've settled in, they listen more carefully, and find that they don't understand what people are saying, and that they are, in fact, speaking Welsh. This sparks the delusion that the whole pub has switched to Welsh in order to be disrespectful to the new arrivals.

Why is this misconception so common? It arises, in my opinion, from a combination of English unconscious conceit and inherited paranoia. The conceit because they did, after all, once rule a quarter of the globe, the paranoia because their ancestors, scattered across that empire, worried that conquered servants, speaking their own language, were at best being rude about them or, even worse, planning to cut their throats.

Rest assured, English visitors we wish you no harm. Except, perhaps, during the Six Nations.

Postscript

This post led to a deluge of comments:

- It was confirmed that yes, there is a committee in Aberystwyth which is charged with creating Welsh equivalents to new English words.

- The common English misperception that Wales is full of pubs where the locals speak English until English people enter, when they immediately switch to Welsh, was even more widespread than I realised.

- This led to a more general discussion regarding when bilingual Welsh people speak Welsh, and when English. The common feeling (completely backed by my own experience) is that the Welsh are in fact extremely courteous, always trying to choose the language in which the person to whom they're speaking is most comfortable.

- There were, however, numerous examples of the dangers of assuming that others don't speak Welsh. Welsh speakers in the Dominican Republic, being rude about a person's choice of food, drew the gentle reprimand, 'Tydi o ddim mor ddrwg â mae'n edrych' (It's not as bad as it looks). Others on the Tube taking the mickey about a woman's hat, leading to the even gentler put-down as she got off at her destination, 'Nos da, hogia!' (Good night, lads!). It worked the other way too. Welsh speakers who were mistaken for visitors being hassled in the Tŷ Newydd in Aberdaron or in a pub in Gerlan, were able to make their tormentors aware, in no uncertain terms and in colourful Welsh, of their mistake.

- Being speakers of a relatively niche language can obviously be fun – a café in Athens which claimed to be able to speak every language in the world (it couldn't). A friend's mynah bird taught some very choice Welsh expressions.

- Others' view of Wales was much lamented. The French, who think it's part of England, and even address letters to 'Pays de Galles, Angleterre' or, if they recognise our existence at all, it's only for 'le rugby'. We seem to be better known in the Far East, with our flag being highly reckoned (presumably because of the dragon), and our rugby players idolised.

- Finally, a tip that I found very encouraging. Alcohol, apparently, improves your language skills. Fluency in Welsh beckons!

CHAPTER 10

Then and Now

WHEN I'D FINISHED writing my account of growing up in Pwllheli, and of my family's connections with Llŷn since I left, my wife suggested I return on my own, to have a good look round and see what's changed. Something the administrator of the *Ysgolion Pwllheli & District Schools* Facebook group suggested I should have done before, not after, writing my memoirs. Harsh but fair.

So I identified three days on my phone weather app when there were more suns than clouds, booked a room at the Lion Hotel in Cricieth (the Crown in Pwllheli was full for the foreseeable future), planned a rough itinerary, and set forth from north Staffordshire.

The first thing I noticed, as I drove through Clynnog Fawr, is that somebody had moved its splendid church from the right of the main road to the left, and that the pub has disappeared altogether. Must have taken some doing, I thought! Note – this is a joke. I realised (eventually – I'm not the sharpest knife in the box) that it's the road that has moved, not the church and the pub!

Pwllheli

In Pwllheli I parked in the official car park in the Maes rather than on-street – I'd been warned by a member of the Facebook group about the 'traffic gestapo' who, apparently, hunt in pairs.

220

During my initial walk around town, I identified lots of changes since – and a few survivals from – my childhood:

- What had been the Conservative Club was in the process of becoming a dental practice. I know teeth are important, but this seemed a bit extreme. That said, actual Conservative voters in this part of north Wales were, in my memory, as rare as – well – hen's teeth. So perhaps they don't need a club. And all of us (well, most of us) have teeth.

- Surviving, just off the Maes, was Ensors where I used to get my shoes re-soled.

- Llên Llŷn, on the Maes where my classmate Mac sold Welsh books, had gone.

- Studt's funfair was still at the far end of the Maes, though now a concreted-in permanent resident rather than the seasonal visitor that I think it once was. Its contribution to the town went back, so we were told in school, to Ffair Pen Tymor, the annual hiring fair, though, that was long before my time.

- Where, as kids, we sat on the wall and watched cattle being slaughtered, there now stood the Maes's public conveniences. Impressive, too – not many toilets are topped by a substantial weather vane. Even so, I got some funny looks as I photographed it.

- Crossville's huge garage was no more. I was once told of an Aberdaron bus enthusiast who refused to believe that a building large enough to accommodate a fleet of double-deckers could possibly exist, and was flabbergasted on his first-ever visit to Pwllheli to view this eighth wonder of the world.

- Walking through to Cardiff Road, I saw that the building that housed Brexo was now Cloth World, but the impressive Palladium Cinema was long gone, replaced by the anodyne Jobcentre Plus. Two establishments central to growing up in Pwllheli in the 1960s – the cinema and the coffee bar – consigned to history. Worth a tear or two, at least to us oldies.

- The Post Office looked much the same as it always did, evoking, for me, lovely memories of my days as a Christmas postie.

- Ginge's dad's bike shop was still there (though without the name 'Martin' over the door), and further up, the Police Station, where I'd reported as missing the bike that I'd left outside the Liberal Club, continued to house the constabulary, and was better painted than it was back then. The air-raid siren on its long poles – used to summon the fire brigade – had, however, gone.

- West End Stores seemed admirably unchanged from when I used to fetch paraffin and drool over pocket-knives I couldn't afford. Not many old-fashioned town centre ironmongers have survived the onslaughts of B&Q, Homebase, Screwfix and the rest. As the saying goes: use them or lose them.

- The Whitehall was whiter than once it was, and the outside steps to the loft above the garage from which my brother fell and knocked himself out was now a part of the restaurant and outdoor smoking area.

- On Llŷn Street, the house in which I was born and brought up hadn't changed much, though the removable slate step that covered the coal chute into the cellar was now cemented over. Mr and Mrs Parker's antique shop and the plumbers with a toilet in the window across the road had become private houses.

- From its rear entrance, choked with builders' vans, I could see that Frondeg School was in the process of being demolished. Shame that they couldn't find another use for it.

- The dilapidated end terrace further up Llŷn Street, that

Dad bought for £25 in which to set up his pottery, had now been incorporated into the house next door, though a small hatch to the right was, I think, where he stored his clay.

- Up the path through Pentra Wanc (no giggling please) where cottages had been replaced by parked cars, Penlleiniau School – flats now for many years – was swathed in scaffolding. The little key-safe attached to the wall beside the front door of the schoolhouse where Mum spent the last thirty-five years of her life remained. It was designed to allow Cymorth Llaw helpers to get in without bothering her.

- At the bottom of Salem Terrace, the houses where Charles (doctor) and Cowell (dentist) practised looked much the same as when I timidly passed through their doors as a child.

- Salem chapel was sad. This huge building, which once held sway over the morals and spiritual life of half the town and rang to hellfire preachers and powerful and harmonious hymns, now, with weedy gutters, broken windows, and prominent 'For Sale' sign, looked defeated and ready for demolition. Like a once-powerful bull, head lowered, waiting for the coup de grâce of the matador's sword.

- In St Peter's Church I interrupted the eleven o'clock Communion service – about eight or nine people and the priest in the Lady Chapel. The amazing thing was that, after so many years away, I knew three of the communicants – perhaps even more (you don't like to ask in case you're wrong). I was able to catch up with local news, swap anecdotes, and take pictures – of the church, the organ my father played, and the plaque commemorating him. Somebody commented that I look like my dad. I'll take that.

- Down Church Street, left onto the High Street, then right down the alley next to the bank, I passed the Town Hall side door where, as a kid, I'd enjoy a crafty fag on my way to get fish and chips from Penlan Street.

- I had a look at where the Liberal Club once stood – still a snooker hall ('clwb snwcer') but without the political affiliation. I couldn't believe that the attached room (now boarded up) where John the Barber plied his trade, and provided prophylactics, was so small!

- The shop halfway down Penlan Street, where we bought elastic for our taflars, and lines, weights and hooks for crab fishing in the harbour, was still there, and still selling fishing tackle (though now also up-market cameras). I had a word with the owner, and he told me that the shop had been started in the 1970s by his parents D. and E. Hughes. Even this was after my time – perhaps they'd bought it as a going concern.

- The trees, whose rooks' nests once sprayed the road below with dead chicks during every spring storm, have since been felled.

- The railway station was recognisable as such, though partly absorbed by the encroaching café and Home Bargains.

- Bon Marche had become the Pen Cob, a Wetherspoon's pub. Though I used to visit Father Christmas' grotto in Bon Marche as a child, and Mum bought material, thread, tape and stuff there, my adult self was happy that it now sells beer rather than haberdashery.

- Around the corner and down some steps is what was originally the *Liverpool Echo* office. It later became a series of restaurants under various names. I and mates Garnett, Brian and Dave and our wives fairly recently had a reunion in one of them. In another, my brother Chris and I ate an evening meal on the day our mother died. It's now called Tookoos Bar and Bistro, though according to its Facebook page, not for much longer. It's heartbreaking when small businesses founder, taking with them all the hopes and dreams and hard work of their owners. I remember other enterprises over the years that failed to survive – canoeing in the harbour, mini golf on South Beach, various shops in the town – and they didn't face the internet shopping/austerity/Brexit/Covid quadruple-whammy that has wiped out even giants like Woolworths, Topshop and Mothercare.

- Before returning to my car, I was glad to see that newsagent Caxton's is still going strong. I also liked that the fish whose head appears to be coming up through the pavement outside the Mitre has its corresponding tail disappearing into the pavement across the roundabout outside what was the Con Club.

My tour complete, I set off to take a look at outlying parts of the town – Lôn Golff, the beach, Gimblet Rock. I'd happily have done it on foot when I was young, but old age gets us all in the end.

If we're lucky.

I'd thought to stop at Pont Solomon, scene of a childhood escapade with a home-made raft, but there were roadworks, so I pressed on. I headed off Cardiff Road along Lôn Golff.

- My first stop was at Talcymarau Mawr, where my Auntie Eva lived out her final years in a rear ground-floor flat. The building looked spruce and impressive. Having parked up, I followed the footpath (to the left of the house, though I could have sworn it used to be to the right) to the slate bridge 'Pont Llechi'. A lovely walk, and a seriously lovely bridge.

- The rest of Lôn Golff had changed beyond recognition – access to the golf club was now, in effect, through a modern housing estate.

225

- The Recreation Ground, with its rusty turnstiles and malodorous changing rooms, was no more. I have memories of watching Pwllheli and District playing Wrexham (giants of the English League's Fourth Division) in the Welsh Cup (we lost), and also, at an athletics meeting, of a Bangor University student running a mile race with a cigarette hanging from his bottom lip. He came last. The Rec had now been replaced by a big modern sports centre, which I was sure was far more fit for purpose.

- The West End Hotel, with its front lounge, snug and snooker room (and a downstairs bar with music), scene of many post-A Levels celebrations which continued after closing time on the beach, was long gone, replaced by a block of flats. The redevelopment of the Prom has been much criticised, but it looked OK to me.

- The Glan-y-Môr Café, buffed up and quite posh, seemed to have had a new lease of life.

- Gimblet Rock somehow seemed smaller that it did when I was a kid, perhaps because of the build-up of sand and Marram grass on its western edge or of the development of the holiday park to the north. Or maybe it's just that I was a kid, and so much smaller than I am now. I looked at the cleft in the rock that I think we called Crochan Berw Mawr – jumping across it was once a rite of passage. We must have been mad. I considered navigating the wilderness of broken rock to look at Crochan Berw Bach, which used to hurl huge columns of spray into the air on stormy days, but decided that at my age it would be asking for trouble. As my daughter has observed, 'falling' is something young people do, whereas we oldies 'have falls' which often lead to broken bones, pneumonia and death.

- I then drove back through Morfa'r Garreg and down the Cob, stopping to look at how the partial reconstruction of Pont Pen y Cob (carried out, according to a plaque, in 1997) has made it safer – little kids can no longer get under the bridge to sit on the tidal gates. The other side of the bridge, where we fished for crabs, was unkempt and overgrown, but the sewage pipe on which we often sat, and sometimes crossed to the Maes, the funfair and the slaughterhouse, looked much the same. Ah! Sewage pipe! Slaughterhouse! The joys of nostalgia!

- Continuing around the harbour, I struggled to recognise where the Legion and Drill Halls had once stood. Abererch Beach also was hard to place. It appeared that an intergalactic starship had landed where once we struggled through the fine sand of the dunes onto the beach. Not a spacecraft at all, I discovered, but 'Plas Heli Welsh National Sailing Academy and Events Centre'. Very impressive, though I understand it hasn't been welcomed with unalloyed enthusiasm. I must admit to feeling sad at the demise of the little café on the beach, half-sunk in fine sand, where we would queue at the hatch for ice-creams, lollies and cold drinks. The beach itself looked shabby and nothing like the scimitar of white sand, backed by massive, path-threaded sand dunes, fronted by a lagoon of blue, sun-warmed water that I remember. But then it was October.

- As for the whole marina area on both sides of the harbour entrance, I couldn't believe how huge a development it had become, compared to Baines where, for two summers in the '60s, I used to fill up jerry cans of petrol and set off in speedboats skippered by Dick Parry and Billy McGill across the bay to Butlins, to run trips off the beach.

Llŷn

Time to have a quick look at some other parts of Llŷn. Growing up, most of my experience was of the south coast. In my memory, at least, it had a Mediterranean feel – blue sea, golden sands, headlands and islands, white-painted houses; even what looked like palm trees in the gardens of prosperous bungalows. And the holiday atmosphere was everywhere – the middle-class yachting incursions into Pwllheli, the almost tropical walk down to the Llanbedrog beach, the total watersports and beach-party scene of Abersoch's gin and Jaguar belt, the surfers in Hell's Mouth. It made it all feel (don't laugh) like the South of France.

My teenage knowledge of the north coast was limited to boozy beach-hut break-ins in Nefyn, traumatic golf rounds along the terrifying cliffs of Morfa Nefyn's links, and a night spent smoking (just cigarettes, not wacky backy) and telling jokes in a caravan perched above the sea somewhere between or beyond Edeyrn and Tudweiliog. In other words, I knew nothing much about what the north coast of Llŷn was really like.

I went some way towards putting this right on my visit. The north coast seemed older, harder, more austere, more Welsh than the south: the string of hills – Yr Eifl, Garn Boduan, Garn Fadryn – each with its Iron Age hill fort; the giant stepped quarries at Trefor and Nant Gwrtheyrn.

Trefor

- Turning off the main A499, I realised that in all the eighteen years that I'd lived in Pwllheli, and all the times I'd visited since, I'd never actually been to Trefor. The reasons are, I suppose, obvious – it's on a loop off the main road, and therefore not on the way to anywhere else, and, more importantly, it didn't have a pub. Yet I knew kids in school and at least one teacher who were from Trefor (Dewi Williams? Mac? Maldwyn?). And Trefor punched well above its weight when it came to the number of comments posted on our Facebook group. So I felt that I owed it a visit.

- I was on the lookout for things I'd learned from the group – for the school where the big kids played something called 'tic petis' in the toilets, the Traeth (beach) where children could swim from the pier and from boat to boat, looking down, through limpid water, at starfish on the seabed below.

- Trefor looked exactly what it is – a quarry town, built of the same stone as was hewn out of the mountain above it. A stream cut through the village, lined with quarrymen's houses, and there was that school, a shop, and a couple of chapels. In the centre I came to a real blast from the past – a car park full of Clynnog & Trefor coaches, together with the company's offices. In my day Clynnog & Trefor played second fiddle to Crossville, with buses that had often seen better days, but the coaches on show here were sleek and up to date.

- I drove down to the beach – a crescent of sand protected by a handsome stone quay, with boats dotted around, at anchor or pulled up on the shore. A man stopped to chat about photography (I was taking pictures), telling me he was born and bred in Trefor, but that his father was Irish, and had come over to work in the quarry. He was on his way out to his boat, and hoped that after a longish layoff the engine would start. Its coughing and spluttering drifted across the water as I drove away.

Nant Gwrtheyrn

Back up to the main road, I set off for Nant Gwrtheyrn, and the language centre housed in the remains of an abandoned village.

The Welsh Language and Heritage Centre had developed out of all recognition since my last visit. The buildings looked immaculate; there were excellent information boards explaining the work that had been done in the village before the quarry closed, and the new Caffi Meinir was a picture, with wonderful views of the sea and headlands. I'd remembered that the hill down to the village was steep, but I hadn't remembered quite how steep. A notice board at the top of the hill said that it was a twenty-five minute walk to the centre. A sight more in the opposite direction, I thought. As I drove back towards Llithfaen, I felt ashamed at how little effort I've made, throughout my life, to convert my imperfect Welsh into fluency. Too late now – I'm seventy-five. If St Peter at the gates of heaven quizzes me in Welsh, I'm sunk!

Nefyn

Through Llithfaen and Pistyll to Nefyn. The town itself and the road down to the beach didn't look much different, but the beach itself seemed to have suffered badly from the landslides that have plagued it. I remember the one in 2001 (and being scandalised when the BBC news placed Nefyn as 'near Holyhead') but I'd completely missed the 2021 one (just six months before my visit).

Cricieth

Of all the towns on Llŷn that are not Pwllheli (and now we're back to the south coast), Cricieth is my favourite. It started with underage drinking and going to dances at the Memorial Hall, and continued when I returned with children and later grandchildren to swim, play on the beach, buy ice-creams in Cadwaladers, and eat in the Blue China. But it's not just that – what's not to like? It's pretty as a picture, with the castle on a hill separating its two bays and beaches and its tight settlement of houses against a backdrop of mountains that sweep south around Cardigan Bay.

At first nothing seemed to have changed – the main streets, the Memorial Hall, the railway crossing, the prom, the lifeboat station, the castle – all seemed exactly like they did when I was a teenager. And, indeed, Cricieth seemed to have weathered the economic storms of the last twenty years far more successfully than many towns in the UK. But there were signs of wear – the Lion (where I was staying) and the George were open only to residents, the Castle (it was The Railway to us) wasn't open at all. 'Everybody's struggling to get staff,' I was told by the young woman who signed me in at the Lion.

For old time's sake I had a pint in the Brynhir, and several in the Prince of Wales. Walking down to the beach as evening fell, most of the houses and businesses seemed in good order. And the castle on its hill silhouetted against a spectacular sunset, together with the view of the sea and the mountains beyond were, as ever, magnificent.

Some people feel that Cricieth is a little twee. A bit too pleased with itself. Not me. Cricieth's lovely!

*

And so, I reflected, as I drove back towards the border with England, is the whole of the Llŷn Peninsula – its towns and villages, its beaches and hills and farms, its bays and headlands and islands, its language and history. It's people.

But, having been born and bred there, I suppose I was bound to think that!

Postscript

Comments consisted of a mixture of further memories and one or two corrections:

- Even residents of Clynnog, I was told, find the layout of the new road disorientating.
- Llên Llŷn, which I thought had disappeared, has simply

migrated – about fifty yards to the shops next to the Mitre. And running it is (roll of drums), Mac's son!

- My use of 'Brexo' for the Expresso Coffee Bar was queried, on the grounds that surely it was 'Espresso'. I checked with Doran, owner Now's wife (and my friend Garnett's sister), and she confirmed that it was Expresso, not Espresso, and that the common abbreviation was 'Brexo'.

- A number of people remembered there being kennels for stray dogs behind the police station, a magnet for tender-hearted children. The police were, apparently, happy to allow local kids to take the dogs home, and two stories told of the effects of this policy. One was of a dog, taken to Abererch Beach, launching itself into the wide blue yonder as soon as it was let off the leash, and defying attempts at recapture. The other was of a dog which escaped its temporary home in Llanaelhaearn, headed straight for the nearest farmer's field and proceeded to herd all of its sheep into one corner. I don't remember dog kennels at the police station – it must have been before or after my time.

- Pont Llechi is obviously held in great affection by those who know it; Plas Heli isn't.

- I was badly mistaken in two respects concerning my first visit to Trefor. The school I saw is not the original one where the kids played 'tic petis', and the stone quay is not the pier that the kids loved to swim from. The demolition of both the old school and the wooden pier were regarded as serious 'how dare they' moments among exiled Treforians!

- Several bathers confirmed that the sea off the north coast is colder than it is off the south. This led to the view that the inhabitants of north Llŷn are hardy souls who are tough as old boots, whilst those of the south aren't!

Epilogue

A note about nostalgia

When, years ago, I first joined Facebook and started reading posts in a variety of groups, I felt a bit uncomfortable about the high nostalgia content. Wasn't nostalgia simply a stick which we oldies use to beat the present? In nostalgia mode, weren't we just saying, to our children and grandchildren, that everything was so much better when we were young? Life was good! We were happy! Our music was superior, our clothes were more stylish, we were cleverer and better looking!

Or were we simply reacting to the young who mercilessly mocked our flares, mini-skirts and Zapata moustaches, laughed at our pathetic lack of tech-savvy, and claimed, with justification, that we had it easy, with our student grants and full employment. Could it be, even, that we weren't nostalgic for the time and place in which we grew up, just for being young?

Then a newspaper article drew my attention to the work of two academics at Southampton University, one Greek, the other Dutch. Exiles themselves, their study of nostalgia was very persuasive. Its bad name, they claimed, goes back to the fact that, in the seventeenth century, homesickness amongst highly-prized Swiss mercenaries was so powerful that it made them useless as soldiers – to such an extent that they had to be written off and sent home to their mountains and pastures. This reputation – as a 'bad thing', even an illness – lasted up to the start of the twenty-first century.

Their research however casts an entirely different light on nostalgia. It is, they claim, a 'good thing'! It encourages empathy and social connectedness, it can combat loneliness, alienation, feelings of meaninglessness or discontinuity between past and present. It can be a positive force for emotional equilibrium, it grounds you and gives you a base from which to evaluate the present as temporary, and perhaps builds resilience. They have even gone so far as to say that nostalgia might be a useful tool in dealing with the effects of trauma, and is already widely seen as a way of treating dementia.

This was a huge relief. After all, nostalgia is, among us Welsh, a part of our national character. We even have a specific word for our longing for our homeland – 'hiraeth'. So let's hear it for nostalgia!

A note about nationalism

I'm proud to be Welsh. Yet there's something about nationalism that, like nostalgia, makes me uncomfortable. I smile indulgently if I pass a car or a house displaying a Welsh flag. Yet I cringe at a car or a house boasting a Union Jack. Why is this? What's the difference?

First, the Union Jack. On reflection, I've come to the conclusion that:

1. The Union Jack has been hijacked (no pun intended) by the political right. It has become associated with the National Front and other extreme right-wing parties, with people who attack fellow citizens of a different colour, who tell people speaking a different language, or English with a different accent, to 'go home', with thugs.

2. I associate the Union Jack, too, with extremely rich, privately-educated, entitled, well-connected people who use it to stir up the masses for their own ends, masses for whom they have nothing but contempt, but who

they see as a useful tool with which to maintain their political ascendancy, and keep their hands on their ill-gotten gains. Which, incidentally, they have already transferred, or will surely in future, transfer, out of this country at the slightest whiff of a threat, at the very drop of a socialist hat, or even at the offer of marginally higher yields elsewhere in the world.

3. The Union Jack represents, not only the UK, but the British Empire. And, by and large, the flags of imperial nations will always represent oppression and exploitation – certainly, to myself, a Welshman and to my wife, a Cypriot.

Now to the Welsh Dragon. My thoughts are:

1. As far as I know, the Welsh flag is not associated with the political right. I've always assumed that Welsh Nationalism is left of centre.

2. By and large, in Wales the entitled rich, the owners of land and resources, the class with their boots on the necks of the poor, have usually been the English, or those who sadly, ape them. Represented by the Union Jack.

3. Wales has never conquered or subjugated other countries. We colonised parts of Patagonia, true, but to my knowledge never attempted to take over Argentina.

As for the look of the two national flags, I'd have to say that both are rather beautiful. But – unbiased opinion – the Welsh dragon beats the Union Jack into a cocked hat. As for national anthems, just listen to 'Hen Wlad fy Nhadau' and 'God Save the Queen'.

The first is inspirational, the second – isn't.

A summing up

It started as a bit of fun – posting miscellaneous memories of growing up in Pwllheli in the mid-twentieth century, and enjoying the resulting comments and anecdotes of other members of the group. Visiting our small Facebook group was like sitting in a virtual pub (or, if you're teetotal, a virtual café or tea room), swapping stories about the old days, making connections, reviving memories, having a laugh. Even making friends, though most of us have never met – after all, we've got only the haziest idea of where we all actually live.

But to us members of the *Ysgolion Pwllheli & District Schools*, I think it became more than that:

- We've heard from the children of teachers who taught us, the children of friends we grew up with, the children of people who employed us. So our reminiscing is clearly not just of interest to ourselves, but to subsequent generations of residents of Pwllheli and the Llŷn Peninsula.

- We've been kept up to date, by those who still live in Llŷn, with changes that have happened since we left.

- We've bonded when Wales won the Triple Crown and the Six Nations, commiserated when they failed to win the Grand Slam.

- We've perhaps begun to appreciate how lucky we were to have been brought up on the Llŷn Peninsula.

- Some of us, especially those of us living in exile, have come to appreciate belonging to a small nation blessed with beautiful countryside, its own language, an impressive history and an ancient culture, all of which sets it, and us, aside from the rest of the world. Distance, as they say, brings perspective.

- For myself, I've also come to embrace, rather than be suspicious of, nostalgia and nationalism, as long as each is used to boost equilibrium and sense of self, and to appreciate and not denigrate the present, and the virtues of other nations.

I'll finish with an exchange attached to one of my original

1970s photographs, posted to the 'Old Pictures of Pwllheli' group. It made me laugh.

The picture shows a lady and a child feeding swans in the harbour from the Pencob bridge. The exchange was prompted by the background, where the gasometers of the old gasworks were clearly visible.

To paraphrase:

First comment: 'I used to fetch a bag of coke from the gasworks for my Nain and carry it home to her in an old pram.'

Second comment: 'I *dream* of owning a bag of coke big enough for me to need an old pram to shift it.'

Acknowledgements

HEARTFELT THANKS TO all who have contributed to the writing of this book:

At Y Lolfa:
- To Lefi Gruffudd for agreeing to publish it, and for answering my initial queries fully, even when he was on holiday.
- To Eirian Jones, not only for detailed and sympathetic editing, but also for advice and encouragement, and wrestling with my mangled Welsh.
- To Gwenllian Jones for sound guidance on all aspects of marketing.

At the *Ysgolion Pwllheli and District Schools* Facebook group:
- To 'she who must be obeyed' Janet Kaiser, the founder and administrator of the group, for her encyclopaedic knowledge of this part of north Wales, for support, encouragement and friendship, and for contributing an excellent (and very flattering!) Foreword.
- To members of the group for their outpouring of stories, anecdotes, memories, jokes, and insights. Above all for their belief that this was a tale worth telling, worth recording and worth remembering. I wish I could have acknowledged everybody by name, but there just wasn't the room!

At other north Wales Facebook groups:
To all those at Facebook groups *Old Pictures of Pwllheli* and *Hiraeth Gogledd Cymru* who 'liked' my pictures of the Llŷn

Peninsula, many taken twenty years ago and, when asked, told me when they were back-to-front.

Also:

- To Simon van de Put, for allowing me to use, on the front cover and free of charge, one of his beautiful paintings of Pwllheli.
- To all the friends and acquaintances of my childhood – I hope you don't mind being mentioned by name, and that your families enjoy the stories (if they hadn't heard them already!).
- To my children (Daniel and Catherine) and grandchildren (Lazaros, Niko and Arianwen), who enlivened the photographs of our numerous family holidays in north Wales, and chipped in with some vivid memories.
- To my wife Doulla who, with good grace, put up with all my maudlin *hiraeth* and did a first invaluable read-through of the manuscript.
- To my brother Chris who gave me not only a younger perspective, but also a wealth of stories that he'd picked up from our mother after I'd flown the nest.
- Above all, to the people of Llŷn in general, and Pwllheli in particular, for giving me such a memorable childhood and, hopefully, for buying this book in huge numbers!

Ask for a print quote!
www.ylolfa.com